SITTING
STILL

Patricia Hart Clifford

PAULIST PRESS
New York, NY• Mahwah, NJ

Cover photo courtesy of Zen Mountain Monastery Archives, Mount Tremper, NY.

Cover design by Tim McKeen.

Library of Congress Cataloging-in-Publication Data

Clifford, Patricia Hart, 1944-
    Sitting still / Patricia Hart Clifford.
        p.   cm.
    Includes bibliographical references.
    ISBN 0-8091-3617-1 (paper); 0-8091-0470-9 (cloth)
        1. Retreats. 2. Contemplation. 3. Meditation—Zen Buddhism. 4.
Clifford, Patricia Hart, 1944-. I. Title.
BV5068.R4C57   1994
269'.6—dc20
                                                      94-15862
                                                          CIP

Published by Paulist Press
997 Macarthur Boulevard
Mahwah, New Jersey 07430

Printed and bound in the
United States of America

CONTENTS

To Thomas G. Hand, S.J.
for his wisdom and courage in pursuing the
truth wherever he found it.

ACKNOWLEDGMENTS

For encouraging me to write this book and providing helpful feedback on the manuscript, I thank Caroline Breedlove, George Clifford, Gita Dedek, Marie Faust Evitt, Karen Jessen, Carolyn Kennedy, Hazel Lane, Ann Saxton Reh, Ruth Sherer, and Lora R. Smith.

I am also grateful to the retreatants who, in questionnaires and interviews, were willing to join me in the struggle to put their experiences with meditation into words. I appreciate their thoughtful responses and their companionship on the journey.

And I warmly thank the Sisters of Mercy in Burlingame, California, who put their vision into action to make these retreats possible.

Introduction

For sheer adventure, exploring the inner space of the human spirit has to equal the exploration of outer space. Inner space holds a realm of existence not readily apparent when we are in the grip of the strident external world. A powerful launching vehicle for the discovery of the realm within is silence. It is in the vessel of silence that inner transformation can occur.

The passage is not an easy one. Just taking the time to sit in quiet meditation requires shutting out all external demands. Even then, every form of internal resistance appears. When the expected tranquility doesn't materialize, it is tempting to give up the effort. I recorded these experiences to show how the difficulties that occur during meditation form a critical part of the journey. It is not sitting in constant bliss but confronting the inevitable obstacles that brings about genuine growth and change.

My own introduction to meditation came many years ago in a university extension class led by a Hindu teacher who taught the mental repetition of a Christian prayer. This experience may explain my easy acceptance of the compatibility of Eastern and Western teachings on the contemplative level. Years later, I became attracted to the simplicity of Zen meditation practice and the wisdom about this practice that has developed over the centuries.

As an active member of a Christian church who also practiced Zen, however, I felt a bit divided despite my conviction about their underlying interconnection. I also

1

needed guidance in how to walk these diverse paths. It
was in a Catholic retreat center with a meditation program
integrating Zen practices with the Christian contemplative
tradition that I found the teaching and support I was looking for and a spiritual home.

In a former convent set against the hills of the San
Francisco Peninsula, the Sisters of Mercy offer an array of
workshops and retreats fostering spiritual growth for people of all faiths. The meditation program at Mercy Center
is led by Jesuit priest, Thomas G. Hand, who uses Zen
teachings he learned in Japan to illuminate the relatively
undeveloped contemplative dimension of Christianity.
This book is the story of a week-long meditation retreat at
Mercy Center.

My intention is to relate the experience of what happens
in meditation. The explanations about why it happens I
leave to the theologians. This is because the focus of the
contemplative path is on inner experience rather than on
theology or beliefs. It is the mystical or contemplative
approach to set aside conventional ways of speaking and
thinking about God or ultimate reality. This is what makes
it possible for those of different religious beliefs to meditate together in a common quest for experiential knowledge of the deepest spiritual truth. In particular at Mercy
Center, it allows Father Hand to use the practices of Zen to
encourage fuller contact with the infinite God beyond religious language and forms.

Along with my own story, I include comments made to
me after the week by eleven other retreatants through
questionnaires and interviews. I also gleaned much from
conversations with others following subsequent meditation retreats. These participants came from a variety of
religious backgrounds. Many were Protestants or
Catholics who turned to Transcendental Meditation, Yoga,
or Buddhism because they didn't find contemplative

forms of spirituality taught or encouraged in their congregations. At Mercy Center they discovered that they did not have to abandon their Christian faith to practice meditation, even when the practices come from Zen.

The method of meditation described here is not one more self-improvement technique. In stilling the mind and learning to pay attention to the present moment, we were suspending our culture's drive for constant self-improvement and achievement. What we were seeking was a contemplative approach to life, a way of being.

The quest is not so much about an ideal state called "enlightenment" as it is about plunging into one's interior depths and finding the courage to face whatever is there. This takes loosening the grip of the carefully cultivated public persona and the all-demanding ego to allow the true core of one's being to emerge. This is the part of our being connected to God. Finding and nurturing that connection is an arduous, lifetime endeavor.

Writing about one week in that pursuit is like trying to describe a mountain using only the characteristics of a single stone. But just as the stone contains many of the properties of the mountain, so one week can reveal many of the patterns that arise on the larger journey.

Each individual who embarks on this voyage will have a different experience. This story is not meant to define what is supposed to happen, but to encourage other travelers to listen to the "still, small voice" within themselves. That voice, found in silence, will disclose the direction of each person's unique way.

Most books on meditation are written by masters, Eastern or Western, who have attained some heights of spiritual development. Their descriptions of the view from the mountaintop can be helpful and inspiring. Sometimes, however, lofty aspirations seem to have little bearing on day-to-day reality. And teachers farther along on the path can minimize the struggles that loomed large at the outset.

I write as one slogging along at the base of the mountain, occasionally catching a glimpse of the peak. Mostly I stumble into the mire and pick myself up as I can. I hope that my story will help fellow pilgrims come to view that mire not so much as terrain to avoid as the nature of the trail that leads to the summit.

Ultimately, the discoveries made in solitude come to permeate everything that we do. As a result, for me and the retreatants I talked to, the stillness practiced during the retreat resulted in activity afterwards that was more authentic, more alive than ever before. Instead of fostering a tendency to be passive or withdrawn, the prolonged silence we experienced led to revitalized connections with others and with all of life.

So while this book is an account of withdrawal into silence, it really describes a passage not away from life but deeper into the heart of it. Solitude and action make up inseparable aspects of the human spirit. Together they allow us to realize the divine reality of our own true nature.

1. Day One: What Do You Seek?

A neat row of empty shoes lined the corridor, toes touching the wall. Placing my sandals at the end of the row, I followed the procession of bare feet through the doorway. To the striking of the wooden drum, we each padded to the center of the room and made a bow to the cross on the Japanese altar. Then we fanned out to our places where we made another bow and took a position for meditation.

Most either sat cross-legged or knelt on round Zen meditation cushions called *zafus*. Some sat on low wooden prayer benches or on chairs. When everyone was settled, the drum beat the rhythm to the song of a deep voice chanting, "Leave all things you have and come and follow me." All of our voices joined together in repeating the chant. When the last drawn-out note had faded, three deep rings of a gong signalled the beginning of silence.

I closed my eyes and took a deep breath. The scent of incense along with the chanting and the reverberations of the gong were intended to create an atmosphere of tranquility, but my mind was in turmoil over what I had gotten myself into. I was one of twenty-five people who had come to this place to meditate six hours a day for seven days. The rest of the time we were to live in silence, like monks. I had always been intrigued by the idea of monastic existence. Now all I could think about was whether I would make it through the week without falling asleep on my *zafu* or going berserk in the quiet.

I tried to recall how this all began. It was in the early seventies when I signed up for a meditation class. I was seeking a calm center in the midst of the stresses of my first teaching job and readjustment to a husband just back from Vietnam. The blossoming Western interest in Eastern religions led me to explore their promise of serenity and answers to life's insoluble mysteries.

I was attracted by the emphasis in Eastern philosophy on what *is* rather than on what *should be*. It offered an antidote to my Protestant upbringing that seemed to require a moral perfection I never could muster. Beginning with the commandment to love my neighbor as myself, these "shoulds" always made me feel that I could never quite measure up, never do enough.

I had left the church I grew up in when I went away to college. But I was unwilling to commit myself to the dogma and regimentation of the Eastern religions I encountered. Without the structure of a group and guidance of a teacher, my meditation practice was sporadic and without direction. Eventually, I became active in the Episcopal church, but in its emphasis on intellectual and social activity I missed the contemplative dimension. It seemed to me that while Christians talked a great deal about faith in God, they tended to act as if salvation depends on words and deeds. Zen Buddhists, on the other hand, did not talk about God, but in the practice of sitting still, demonstrated the extremities of faith.

Over the years, I became increasingly aware of how my Sunday School "shoulds" had been reinforced by an upbringing in the fifties concerned with the approval of others and "doing the right thing." This emphasis on appearances and fitting in required a suppression of my interior self. As a result, I felt that I didn't know who I really was. I had a persistent sense that time was passing and I was missing out on something essential.

When I looked back over my life, I found that my most memorable moments were of times I was sitting still—listening to the rustle of leaves in a breeze or the splashing of a mountain stream. All the rushing around I had done in pursuit of external goals was just a blur. Hours, days, months, and years had been swallowed up in that blur. Only when I stopped did I become something more than the sum of my doing.

I had come to this retreat to rediscover what I had glimpsed in those times of stillness. I wanted to learn to live that way all the time — with wholehearted absorption in the moment rather than just going through the motions. To do this I knew I had to leave the vociferous demands of the outside world behind in order to plunge into the core of my being.

The day before, I had seen my daughter off to summer camp, kissed my husband good-bye and made the forty-minute drive north to Mercy Center in Burlingame, California. There I drove through iron entry gates and past ancient oaks filtering the late afternoon sun. Beds of Iceland poppies in shades of pink, lemon, and tangerine lined the walkway leading to the massive wooden entry doors of the sprawling former convent.

After registering, I unpacked in a narrow, austere room on the fourth floor. A closet, sink, and small desk lined one wall opposite a bed and an armchair. No telephone, radio, television, or computer intruded on the simplicity of this tiny space. With my belongings pared down to toiletries and a few comfortable clothes, I began to feel relief from the complexities of daily existence.

From the window at one end of the room I could look down on the wooded creek that separates the forty acres of retreat center grounds from the residential neighbor-

hood surrounding it. Beyond the treetops and rooftops I
saw the mountain with the giant white letters on it
spelling out "South San Francisco. The Industrial City."
When I opened the window the sound of rock music
blared into my room from one of the backyards across the
creek, hinting that the outside world couldn't be escaped
entirely.

After dinner, our group gathered in a circle of comfortable chairs and sofas lining a spacious meeting room. We
introduced ourselves only by name and where we lived in
order to begin not identifying ourselves by what we do.
Ages ranged from the twenties through the seventies,
with most appearing to be in their forties and fifties.
Women predominated in the group; only five of the twenty-five were men. Several prefaced their names during the
introductions with "Sister" and one with "Brother" of religious orders.

The retreat director, Jesuit priest Tom Hand, introduced
himself and explained how he came to be there. This soft-
spoken, white-haired man in his early seventies lived for
twenty-nine years in Japan, teaching English to Japanese,
and leading Catholic retreats. For the last six of those
years he received formal training in Zen practice. When he
returned to the United States, he began incorporating
what he had learned into the Christian contemplative tradition.

Father Hand told us that his Jesuit education had
emphasized theology and ethics, with little attention
given to the spiritual life of the individual. This deficit
spurred his interest in the experiential focus of Zen. That
training in Japan always placed doctrine secondary to
practical instructions for meditation and for living.

When Father Hand returned to the United States in
1984, the Sisters of Mercy invited him to bring this Eastern
approach to spirituality to their retreat center. He began

with conferences on Buddhist-Christian dialogue and a day of meditation on the last Sunday of each month. When interest grew, he added daily morning and weekly evening meditation sessions, then weekend and week-long retreats.

After relating this background, Father Hand introduced Chiao-Lin, who would be assisting him during the week. This diminutive young woman with long, black hair had recently moved to this country from Taiwan. Apologizing for her heavily accented English, Chiao-Lin told us that she had spent the previous week at a rigorous retreat in *vipassana*, or Insight, meditation.

Father Hand then gave us instructions for the week. We were to choose a simple focus for our attention during meditation, such as a word or our breath. This focal point is not something to think about but is used to quiet the mind. We still the senses, memory, reasoning, and physical movement in order to let in an awareness of the infinite. Father Hand said that the experience we seek was called by the unknown fourteenth-century author of the *Cloud of Unknowing*, "the stirring of the heart."

This is not the heart associated with emotions which, like thoughts, are to be let go without judgment when they arise. Everything associated with the self is to be let go. "Self-forgetfulness, which brings us to the very center of our being, is associated with the Biblical concept of heart," relates Brother David Steindl-Rast in *Speaking of Silence*. "The heart is where we are fully alive, fully aware, fully ourselves... where the human and the divine are simply one."

I chose to count my exhalations up to the number ten, then start again with one. I had found that the counting helped return my attention to my breath when my mind wandered. In that first evening meditation session of the retreat, every time I was distracted from counting, I would return to the number one. Anxious thoughts about the coming week were so persistent that when the gong signalled the end of the first twenty-five minute period, I had not passed the number four.

At that sound of the gong, we all rose in unison and began five minutes of *kinhin*, or walking meditation. Circling very slowly in a single file around the front row of *zafus* and back row of chairs, I tried to focus on the act of walking. My eyes drifted to those on the other half of the room who were making an identical circuit around their seats as my thoughts continued to churn. Whenever I noticed that I had taken a step with my mind elsewhere, I would direct my attention back to the sensation of the soles of my feet touching the floor.

The room we were in fostered serenity. At the front, a tall Japanese altar of light-colored wood framed a plain dark wooden cross flanked by candles. Recesses below the cross held a small pottery bowl containing the incense and a plaque with the Japanese character for "Mu" in calligraphy. In Zen, "Mu" signifies the way to ultimate truth through the emptying of self. In this way it is analogous to the empty cross. Together they gave notice that a surrender of self would be required here.

An arrangement of rocks in sand in one corner of the room and Chinese brush paintings on the walls contributed to the atmosphere of a Zen meditation hall. Characters in Chinese calligraphy on one small scroll represented the word "zabodo." "Za," Father Hand had told us, "means sit, 'bo' means forget, and 'do' means hall. So this room is a hall in which to sit and forget." This coincides with the instructions in the *Cloud of Unknowing* to put a "cloud of forgetting beneath you, between you and all the creatures that have ever been made."

The ringing of a little bell ended the walking period, and we all settled ourselves for a second twenty-five minutes of meditation. Jet engines of a plane taking off from the nearby San Francisco airport rumbled overhead, then only the sounds of breathing remained.

Father Hand had stressed to us the importance of being clear about our purpose in sitting. He told us that at his initial meeting with his Zen master in Japan only one thing was asked and discussed: his intention. He pointed out that when Jesus of Nazareth met his first disciples he asked them, "What do you seek?"

When I interviewed some of the retreatants after the week was over, I asked them that question. Though they expressed what they wanted in different ways, all could be described as wanting something more than just intellectual understanding. What they sought was concrete experience of the reality at the root of their being.

On a *zafu* at the front of the room by the altar sat Ada, her erect posture pulling her tiny frame up to a greater height. In her sixties and recently retired from her job as a software librarian, Ada was born into a family of Orthodox priests in Moldava, then the eastern part of Romania. When her family had to flee their home to escape persecution, she lost her belief in a God that allowed the atrocities she saw in her country.

Ada felt compelled, however, to pursue answers on a spiritual level. When she came to this country she became interested in the religious teachings of Asia and learned to meditate. In this practice she rediscovered the faith she had lost. She told me that she came to Mercy Center because she found the foundation of the truths that speak to her most deeply encompassed there. "For me to believe," she said, "is not easy. I believe not because I see or hear something but because of a faith inside of me. Having faith is a huge gift." She defines what she seeks in meditation as coming to know "the divine Source."

The white-haired woman sitting in the chair behind me

was also drawn here by the integration of Eastern and Western spiritual teachings. Clare's elderly body totters unsteadily during *kinhin*. She told me that for her meditation is a way to seek an understanding of the mystery of life. This was her fifth seven-day retreat here, and she observed, "Meditation makes my life seem all of one piece, less fragmented." A retired psychiatric social worker, Clare also reported that meditation helps her renew the energy she finds flagging as she ages. Some were motivated to make this retreat by particular problems they faced in their lives. Both Linda and Geoff came at a time when they were struggling with career decisions. Geoff had left the seminary where he had been studying for the Presbyterian ministry and was working as a systems analyst. He signed up for the retreat in order to confront the lack of direction he was feeling in his life.

He explained that he wanted to "tap the wisdom of my own inner voices by allowing them to percolate into my awareness. I need meditation," he said, "to remind me of the sacredness of the inner reality that gets lost in the externals of my everyday life." He also wanted to reflect on the relationship between spirituality and social action.

Linda had been an ethics and theology teacher at a Catholic high school who took a job in a department store when the school she taught in closed. With an M.A. in religious education and experience leading retreats in her church, she felt that she had a different calling. She told me that for her the retreat was the next step in discerning her direction. "I wanted to create an extreme situation for myself," she related. "I believe in and need verbal expression and activity, but when it comes to paying attention to my deepest self, what I call bottom line stuff, where I go is to stillness and silence."

Marianne is a marriage and family counselor who came to the retreat from her home in the state of Washington.

She started meditating at the suggestion of her sponsor in a Twelve-Step program. "Meditating daily enabled me to let go of an addictive relationship for the first time in my life," she revealed. "As I continued to meditate, other changes occurred in me, and I became hungry for something I couldn't put my finger on. That hunger led me to this retreat."

"It was being gay that made me a seeker," stated Richard, an attorney in his fifties from the East Coast. "After I figured out I wasn't going to be able to change, I decided to become very serious about my religion." A lifelong Catholic, he immersed himself in the study of his faith. It was hearing an audio tape of a talk by Father Hand that started Richard meditating and brought him here for his first retreat. "My concentration is very poor," he disclosed, "but what I heard Father Hand say on that tape made sense to me and that's the reason I'm here."

Like me, most of these people had also met with incomprehension from those they had told about the retreat. ("No one's talking?" Linda's mother had asked her in disbelief.) While I didn't know any of the others when I arrived and scarcely remembered any names from our brief introductions, their presence offered the reassurance of a shared enterprise. We may not have been talking, but we were decidedly in this together.

When the final gong sounded on that first evening, we were more than just twenty-five individuals here for our own separate purposes. In the air was an unspoken mutual support that made me believe it might be possible to survive the week. There was also a mutual acknowledgment that this retreat was about something greater than ourselves. This gave our diversity a common purpose and created a fellowship in the midst of solitude.

Upstairs in my room, I looked at the schedule. The next two days called for a later start in the morning and fewer meditation sessions than the rest of the week. Even during this transition period, with meals and talks there was very little free time. It seemed strange to me that it would take so much external structure to bring us to the internal freedom that we were seeking. Yet it was freedom that was at the base of what I hoped for here: freedom from shoulds, from periodic anxiety and depression, from overpowering emotions, from illusions — and from the suffering that all this produced.

In my room a pile of books on meditation sat on the little desk. I had brought these to provide bedtime reading and some explanation of how this freedom would come about through stillness and silence. Father Hand, however, had recommended that we not read at all this week except for occasional brief inspirational passages. Reading, he told us, would engage us in ideas, and what we wanted was not ideas but direct experience. Anything that encouraged the activity of the intellect would distract the attention of the heart from its movement toward the infinite.

I left the books untouched and turned off the light. Closing the window did not even muffle the din of the rock music, which had increased in volume from the afternoon. Loud voices confirmed that a large party was now at full throttle across the creek. Unable to complain in the silence and the unfamiliar surroundings, I fumed at the disruption of the evening's tranquil mood and the impediment to sleep. I was certain that the noise would make my fears of dozing off on my cushion the next day a reality.

I tossed in my bed with growing irritation. My shoulds demanded compassion toward my fellow human beings, but I could only conjure up annoyance. This seemed to be an especially inauspicious start for a retreat. Once again I was confronting my failure to love my neighbor. After awhile I remembered Father Hand's admonition not to judge our emotions or our thoughts. At least I could let myself seethe.

At 1:30 a.m. the clamor came to an abrupt stop. Maybe some of the neighbors complained. I glanced at the clock with the alarm set for six. In five hours I would be trying to keep myself upright on my *zafu* and count to ten.

2. Day Two: Breathe In, Breathe Out

My alarm clock clanged for several minutes before I could rouse myself to turn it off. It was not a good night. Although I fell asleep after the party noise stopped, a lumpy mattress and my trepidation about the coming week kept waking me up. Father Hand made it clear that we were expected to be present at all the meditation sessions. If I stayed in bed, my empty *zafu* would be noticed. On the other hand, after less than four hours of slumber my chances of remaining awake through a morning of silence were slim. Sleeping until breakfast and then starting rested seemed like the sensible thing to do.

I closed my eyes and dozed. The sound of footsteps scuffling to and from the bathroom down the hall broke into my drowsy cocoon. Those with rooms on the same side of the building must have been kept awake by the party too, and it sounded as if at least some of them were up. These first two days, I remembered, were the easier ones. I decided that I had better fling my body out of bed for the warm-up or I would never manage the real thing.

I pulled on sweatpants and a T-shirt in the semi-darkness and stumbled down the five flights of stairs to the ground floor. Joining the group for stretching exercises in the meeting room, I began to wake up. When we filed across the hall for our hour of meditation before breakfast, not one place was empty. Peer pressure had its uses. I was just glad I didn't have to talk to anyone.

Instead of beginning with a chant, we started with a visualization exercise. Father Hand said that its purpose was to give us a clearer idea of what we were seeking. He asked us to picture a door, then imagine it opening so we could see what was on the other side. My door opened onto thick fog. An image of Jesus materialized out of the fog, then vanished, and I was left enveloped by an impenetrable grey mist.

I was confused. Did the fog represent the cloud of unknowing — or just haziness from lack of sleep? Was the appearance of Jesus reassurance about letting go of religious images? Even so, the fog made me uneasy about what was in store for the coming week.

When I turned my attention to counting my breaths, the meandering stream of thoughts appeared that had distracted me the night before. The Cistercian monk, Thomas Keating, calls this superficial level of thought "woolgathering" and says it is caused by the imagination's "propensity for perpetual motion." Deeper layers that can be encountered Keating designates as emotions, psychological insights, reflections on the experience, and the dynamics of the unconscious.

The thoughts that distracted me so far were clearly on the surface level of "woolgathering." I heard Geoff, sitting on my left, swallow. This triggered in me the desire to swallow and made me reflect on how noisy this usually unnoticed action sounded in the quiet. I wondered what we would have to eat for breakfast. I speculated about what my daughter was doing at camp. Instead of providing entertainment for my mind, however, these musings only made me bored and restless. It seemed curious that for those fleeting seconds that I *was* able to concentrate on what would seem to be the more tedious occupation of counting my breaths, my mind was serene and without boredom.

Father Hand had told us that our aim was not to stop thinking entirely, an impossible task, but just not to follow the thoughts that inevitably arise. I read after the retreat, in *Speaking of Silence*, a discussion between Christian and Buddhist teachers on the subject of contemplation, that these two traditions are in agreement on the matter of dealing with distracting thoughts in meditation. *Vipassana* teacher Joseph Goldstein observes, "I don't think it is a matter of not thinking. It is a matter of not entering into dialogue with thought." Treating a thought as just another phenomenon like a sound, according to Goldstein, "simplifies the whole process, because then there is not the extra effort to stop thinking." The Eastern Orthodox priest George Timko put it this way, "The way to deal with thought is to watch the mind. If you are watching the mind, it can't fool you.... But by contemplating, by simply watching, the mind naturally becomes quiet and stills itself."

Watching the mind requires a detachment that is tricky to maintain. It's like sitting in a movie theater and trying not to follow the plot of the film on the screen. Every time I'd begin counting my breath, my mind would seize on some scene unfolding in my imagination, and my breath would be forgotten. When I noticed myself immersed in these dramas, I would grow discouraged about my ability to maintain some modicum of attention.

Settling in after *kinhin*, I glanced around the room and saw serene faces that appeared to be in perfect concentration. A large, blonde woman in the row facing mine sat Buddha-like with a beatific smile. I found out later that her name is Felicite and that she flew out to the retreat from Maryland. Despite her appearance of serenity, she told me that self-criticism over not being able to maintain a focus of attention was a problem for her as well. She said, "When I'm meditating, the issue of how to deal with the inner critic is ever present. To love myself while my mind is wandering all over is a difficult spiritual exercise."

I recognized my inner critic as the part of me that points out where I've failed to live up to my "shoulds." The idea was not to make concentration one more "should" but to observe the self-criticism along with the other thoughts that appeared. Repeatedly identifying and discarding the negative voice seemed to be the only way to rid myself of it.

After a breakfast of fresh fruit and French toast, we assembled in the meeting room for a talk. Father Hand spoke about the opening sentence to the gospel of John, "In the beginning was the Word." "In the beginning," he told us, "means 'at the source of everything', and that Source, that we call God, has no form. The Word or 'Logos' is the manifestation of that Source in a form. Our aim in meditation is to identify ourselves with the Word, that is, to come to know ourselves as a singular, unique manifestation of the formless Source. This is the consciousness of Christ and with it we can apprehend our true identity and loosen our exclusive identification with the narrow ego self."

Discovering this true identity comes not through intellectual understanding but through a shift in consciousness. Father Hand noted that this shift happens in concrete ways that differ with each person. He gave the example of one woman who was focusing on her breathing during a meditation retreat. She told him that in one moment she saw in each breath of her own the breath of all others. "This is the identification of the individual with the whole," he declared, "and brings with it a state of great joy, reverence, and awe. We each come to this awareness in our own individual ways."

When the talk was over, I sat bewildered on the sofa, trying to comprehend how these words applied to me. It finally dawned on me that to persist in mulling it over would be dwelling on ideas, and that was what we were supposed to avoid. It had been made clear that any shift in consciousness would not come about through mental effort. "We are not here to make something happen," Father Hand had informed us, "but to let something happen." I hoped the ideas I'd heard would sort themselves out beneath the level of my conscious mind.

When I returned to meditation, I found one phrase from the talk recurring in my mind: "I am a singular, unique manifestation of God." My "woolgathering" had become interspersed with what Thomas Keating would call "insight." I put the rest of the ideas aside, something that Richard told me later he was not able to do. He said he became so absorbed in the concepts from the talks during the week that he found himself pondering them frequently during meditation.

During this first day's sessions, Father Hand began meeting with us individually in order to check that we each had a clearly defined focal point on which to meditate. When Geoff returned to his *zafu* next to mine, I got up and went across the hall, where I described my difficulties in getting to ten. Father Hand suggested that I shift my attention from a preoccupation with the numbers to concentration on the breath itself.

I told him about my visualization of the fog. His comment was, "We need words and images to learn about the Christ, but we need to let go of the words and images to become one with Christ. The fog is a movement toward that oneness." I took this encouragement back with me to my cushion.

There I redirected my attention to the sensations of air entering and leaving my nostrils. I saw that I had been really just playing games with the numbers before, trying to see how high I could count before my mind wandered. Paying attention to my actual breaths gave me something more tangible to focus on and helped minimize the duration of my mental excursions.

While Father Hand was holding these individual conferences, Chiao-Lin led the meditation periods. This tiny woman appeared to sit and walk with perfect concentration. She struck the little bell to bring us back from distractions at exactly the moment I needed the bell. The few admonitions she offered always addressed my immediate plight. "Be alert," she exhorted us when I was feeling sluggish. And when my awareness of the sensations of breathing became vague, I'd hear, "No matter what your focus, make it clear and sharp."

After a noisy crash of dishes from the kitchen on the floor above us, she calmly asked, "Will you let yourself be distracted by a few kitchen noises? How easily then you will be shaken by the distractions of the world." During *kinhin*, when my eyes roamed the room, I noticed Chiao-Lin's unwavering lowered eyelids and remembered our instructions not to look around while walking. I began keeping my eyes on the carpet.

Before lunch many of our group gathered for mass in the cavernous chapel. Standing around the altar in a circle, we turned to the age-old act of breaking bread and drinking wine. Like watching the breath in meditation, this ritual focused our attention on the ordinary and invited us to see something in it that we usually miss. I remembered Father Hand's words, "Through awareness of particular forms, we come to know the Formless."

When I left the chapel, it dawned on me that I had not felt sleepy all morning. During the free time after lunch, however, I fell asleep for an hour, waking up just before the first afternoon meditation session. All that fury I had expended on the party-goers last night came from anticipating drowsiness that didn't materialize. I recognized this scenario that is repeated often in my life: aggravation over some anticipated problem that never occurs.

Between afternoon meditation sessions, we gathered to watch a video Father Hand had recorded from Japanese television. When we thought we would have to listen to the narrative in a language we didn't understand, Linda and I exchanged grimaces. In this kind of situation it was the toughest to resist making an offhand remark to a person nearby. I had to settle for making faces. Chiao-Lin told us later in the week that the group at her *vipassana* retreat was instructed to avoid even eye contact with each other to minimize all forms of interaction.

When the video began, Father Hand turned off the volume and provided an English commentary for the pictures. It was a documentary about people making pilgrimages to Mt. Kailas, a 22,027 foot mountain in Tibet sacred to Buddhists, Hindus, and the Tibetan Bon people. The pilgrims interviewed said that they climb to the base of the peak and circumambulate it in order to earn merit so that they can improve their station in lives to come. Surely, I thought, there must be grace, too, in the pilgrimage itself. These people take years of their lives to make the arduous journey. Many encircled the peak several times, some prostrating themselves each step of the way.

A pilgrimage seemed to be defined by arduousness. The trek around a 22,000 foot mountain takes the same kind of single-minded dedication and the same foolhardy, irrational faith as sitting on a cushion for six hours a day. Yet even in a video it was easy to see how anyone might believe that gods reside on the imposing peak of Mt.

Kailas. This seemed to make more sense, in fact, than looking for the divine in my mental fog.

After the video, Father Hand began the next meditation session with a relaxation exercise. He told us that one of the main reasons for lack of progress in meditation is physical tension. While many people think that meditation is done in order to relax, we actually must relax in order to meditate. We began with a deep breath, then followed his directions to release tension in the scalp, face, and jaw, all the way down to our toes. I discovered several tense muscles in my neck and shoulders.

Before dinner, the aroma of food being prepared wafted through the high windows of the Rose Room and mingled with the sweet fragrance of the incense. The silence settled around me like a cape that I was becoming accustomed to wearing. Very briefly, I sensed the possibility of a common identity among all of us, that we all might breathe as one. Then someone coughed and my feeling of separation returned. I breathed a little more easily though until the gong rang out dinnertime.

Father Hand had recommended that we eat less than usual during the week because meditation is hampered when a great deal of energy must go into digestion. We were also using up fewer calories than usual with so much sitting. After hearing this, I was startled when I arrived at dinner ravenous. When I cleared my plate of the fried chicken, rice pilaf, and vegetables, I wanted seconds. After finishing the seconds, I helped myself to one of the larger squares of chocolate cake. I couldn't tell whether I was eating more than usual out of hunger or out of fear of becoming hungry later. It was as if some primitive survival instinct had kicked in that told me to fill up in the face of the unknown.

After dinner, our group met to air any questions we had in a scheduled exception to the silence. Richard asked if it

was acceptable during meditation to move or change position when he was uncomfortable or if his legs hurt. Father
Hand answered that his Zen teacher in Japan had insisted
on no movement whatsoever, but from his own experience he concluded that pain could be more of a distraction
than a help. "Don't move every time you feel uncomfortable," he said, "or you will be shifting around all the time.
But sitting in a lot of pain is not very productive either.
Change your position quietly and all at once if you have
to, then sit still."

Chiao-Lin's *vipassana* training gave her a slightly different view. "If you sit long enough in any position, you will
feel some pain," she said. "If you fight the pain in your
mind, it will stay. If you gently recognize it as you would
any distraction and go on with your concentration, the
pain will go away."

I remembered one time before the retreat when I felt
sleepy during meditation. I took deep breaths, sat up
straighter, and tried harder to concentrate — all in a vain
effort to fight off drowsiness. When I decided to stop
fighting it and let myself be sleepy, I soon found myself
awake and alert.

"If the pain becomes bad enough," Chaio-Lin continued, "you can use it." I asked her what she meant by
using the pain. She replied that pain makes us focus on
what is happening in the present. "When the pain
becomes your focus of attention, it obliterates the thoughts
that are trying to create a more pleasant world in the
mind. When something hurts, you can't escape the reality
of the here and now."

Father Hand reiterated the nonjudgmental nature of
meditation. Pain, sleepiness, a persistent itch, or a distracting noise are not to be viewed as undesirable any more
than a state of serenity or profound insights are to be
viewed as desirable. The reason for dropping the judg-

ments that make up so much of our daily thinking
process, he explained, is that judgment of anything, internal or external, heightens our sense of separation from
what we are judging. What we want is to replace the sub-
ject-object way of perceiving for direct awareness, in
which subject and object become one. In direct awareness
there is no separation between the perceiver and the perceived and therefore no comparison or judgment.

Felicite told me after the retreat that in trying to practice
this kind of nonjudgmental detachment she discovered
how quickly she labels everything she encounters as good
or bad. She considered the roaring of jet engines we frequently heard as disruptive to meditation until she considered the point of view of the passengers on the plane.
When she imagined what those same sounds meant to
those on the way to their destinations, she began to listen
in a different way. "Just to hear the sound and not judge
it," she said, "was a new experience." This was a detachment I hadn't been able to manage with the party noise
the night before.

Marianne asked why we bow. "We bow to the cross on
the altar as a sign of respect for this symbol of faith,"
Father Hand answered. "We bow to our cushion because
that is our own calvary — the place where we die to the
ego self." For me, the bowing was a ritual that marked the
shift from the outer world to the inner world. Nobody can
expect to just dash in, plop down, and concentrate. The
actions of the body help to get the message through to the
mind that it is time to quiet down.

The Zen master Bassui called bowing a "way of hori-
zontalizing the mast of the ego." Like kneeling, it is an act
of humbling oneself. Bassui also said that we bow to each
other "as a sign of mutual respect and identification with
one another's aspiration." The bow to the other acknowl-

edges that we are fellow travelers on the same pilgrimage, like those climbing a mountain together.

After the question period, we walked slowly across the hall, in no hurry to go to our crosses. The pilgrims who encircled Mt. Kailas by prostrating themselves every step of the way were not in a hurry either. Speed, achievement, and success — none of these things so important in the world count on the spiritual journey. Or maybe they count only as they are given up. Already, I had given up hope of making visible progress. Getting out of bed in the morning, paying attention to my breath, resisting the impulse to break the silence with a casual remark to someone — all these seemingly simple acts reflected internal struggles. As with the pilgrims in Tibet, being the first one around the mountain wasn't the point here.

Candles flickered and incense burned in this room that was becoming our Mt. Kailas. In the evening darkness I felt less restless and somewhat elated at surviving the first full day. Breathe in and breathe out. I could do that. My concentration was erratic, but, with my expectations lowered, I could be grateful that I was breathing.

We closed the evening meditation session with prayers for a troubled world, for the suffering, for those we love. We sang a chant from Taizé, the French interdenominational monastic community known for the simple beauty of its music.

> Come and fill our hearts with your peace.
> You alone, O Lord are holy.
> Come and fill our hearts with your peace.
> Alleluia.

We made our final bows of the day, touching our heads to the floor.

In my room I looked out the window at city lights flickering in the distance against the dark mountain. The neighborhood was quiet, spent from last night's revelry. I had a chance at sleep.

The fourth floor was not 22,000 feet, but I felt in rare air nevertheless. I have backpacked enough at high elevations to know the importance of taking a breath with each step under such conditions. Brushing my teeth, I breathed in. Setting my alarm, I breathed out. Standing at the window, breathing goodnight to the quiet neighborhood and the lights of the city, I put aside worries about sleeping well enough to get out of bed in the morning, about making it through the next day. I fell asleep counting my breaths.

3. Day Three: Past and Future

It was the sharp crack of the mallet striking wood that first drew me to Zen. That summons to the meditation practice called *zazen* proclaimed the unmistakable command: "Wake up." An altogether different tone from the mellifluous sound of the gong that followed, the wood offered no mercy. It said: "You must hide nothing. You must be cracked open."

On my *zafu* in the early morning hush, my whole being directed itself against waking up. My restless body squirmed and fidgeted while my mind drifted. Changing my position did not satisfy my body but led to a craving for more movement. In the same way, letting my mind drift did not appease it but only spawned more daydreams.

"We're not here to meditate for a week but to meditate for this moment," Father Hand reminded us at the start of the morning session. The present moment was the one thing that eluded me. When I remembered to watch my thoughts instead of follow them, what I noticed reeling through my mental picture show were random snippets of memories from the past and worries about the future. I would catch the here and now only in a fleeting awareness of inhaled air, then it would slip away in the next reverie.

By the end of the morning, I'd watched enough of these ruminations to classify them into categories. I observed two kinds of thoughts about the past and two about the future. Usually, when a memory from the past surfaced, my mind would replay the event in vivid detail. Sometimes, however, I would embellish a scene, re-creating it to fit the way I wished it had happened. In the re-created scene I always appeared more wise or selfless than I had been at the time. I labeled these "replaying" and "re-creating."

For the future, the idea of an anticipated event would arise, usually one I felt some anxiety about. At other times I would go through a full mental rehearsal of my part in the event, complete with scenes and dialogue. These I labeled "anticipating" and "rehearsing."

Once I had devised these categories, I labeled most thoughts that appeared. This process seemed to provide sufficient detachment for me to avoid becoming too immersed in the diversion. When the thought had a label, it was easier to let it go.

Categorizing thoughts also revealed what a large part of my daily mental activity goes into rehashing the past and worrying about the future. There are, of course, legitimate reasons for ruminating on the past and future, such as the resolving of unsettled issues or the making of specific plans. This is not what I was doing. The scenes I watched streaming through my consciousness had no practical or emotional significance that I could discern. Their overriding purpose appeared to be escape from the present. Without any constructive link to reality, these thoughts formed a barrage of distractions that kept me from living fully in the moment. No wonder I felt as if life were passing me by.

I concluded that I must be reliving the past so much because I didn't fully experience it the first time. If I hadn't been all that attentive when an event occurred, it made sense that I might want to recover what I missed. Thoughts about the future, I decided, reflected my preoccupation with the way things should be. They were an attempt to fulfill some ideal in fantasy if not reality. What produced the anxiety was the possibility of reality not conforming to the fantasy.

During the morning talk, Father Hand read a story that illustrated how one person did experience full attention to the present moment. The author related an incident from his youth when he had been sleeping in a barn before beginning a shift of all-night plowing. He described how, when awakened at midnight, he was awestruck by the dramatically ethereal beauty of his surroundings. The tractor, the moon, and the haystack all took on a magical presence, time seemed to stop, and he was overcome with great joy. He recalled this event when he returned to the same farm many years later to visit his cousin Riley, who had never left.

Riley knew what he was talking about and explained it like this: "To open the senses, to become really conscious, you have to drop out of the future and the past and remain for a time on what T.S. Eliot called 'the still point of the turning world' — the present. The only true reality is the present. The future is not yet." What happened that night in the barn, Riley told his cousin, was that "You stopped planning into the future and thinking about the past. You were there in the now."

Father Hand commented that this kind of experience often happens when one's routine is shaken up in some way, like waking up in a barn at midnight. We had come here to be shaken up, he told us. With our normal routines set aside, we had a chance to shift out of our preoccupation with the past and the future into the still point we were seeking.

What was so intolerable about the present, I wondered, that I couldn't bear it for more than a few seconds at a time? "Living in the present requires accepting yourself as complete in this moment," Father Hand declared. "Otherwise you are always in the process of becoming." It dawned on me that my continual replaying and rehearsing of events reflected a lack of self-acceptance. I was revising the past to improve on what I had said or done and rehearsing the future to ensure a better performance.

Father Hand concluded, "The spiritual basis of self-acceptance is knowledge of our divine nature. Our minds don't accept that we are each the incarnation of the glory of God. We have to come to know it in our hearts, and we can do this through meditation.

"When I went up to my room after the talk, I found a pink slip of paper on my floor. It was for my neighbor Linda, put under my door by mistake. The note confirmed an appointment for a massage from one of the Sisters of Mercy at the Center. I had seen the notice that offered massages posted on the bulletin board but was too overwhelmed by coping with the existing agenda to even consider the intricacies of making a phone call and scheduling an appointment. When I slipped the message under Linda's door, though, I felt the tightness in my neck and shoulders along with new stiffness in my leg muscles and wished that the appointment had been mine.

After the retreat, Linda told me that having a massage was part of a deliberate effort she made during the week to take care of herself, a crucial aspect of self-acceptance. "Making my own choices and not worrying about what others might consider right or wrong was an important part of the retreat for me," she declared. She felt that the silence allowed her to hear and give precedence to her own needs, which are often subjugated to the needs and opinions of others. "The main thing," she asserted, "was to take off the mask and let down, whether that meant not smiling at everyone I passed in the hall, changing my focal point in meditation when I was moved to, or sketching during the breaks. I just decided to be myself."

For me, reveries about the the past and future created a barrier to being myself. All that re-creating and rehearsing was in reality a continual adjusting of my self-image. My ego was working overtime to try and make me into someone I was not.

The purpose of all this effort, I saw, was not just to fool myself but to create an image that I could present to others. From the moment of my arrival I wanted to fit in. If Linda didn't worry about what others thought of her having a massage, I would have. My desire for others to think well of me was becoming apparent in the silence. It was this desire that got me out of bed in the morning and kept me on my cushion. But I could see how my craving for acceptance and approval also kept me from knowing who I really am.

In the afternoon we saw another video from Japanese television, again with a commentary in English from Father Hand. This one showed a *sesshin*, the traditional Zen Buddhist retreat our week was modeled on. The documentary began with a lone aspirant applying to a monastery to be taken in for training. He was made to sit outside on the steps for many hours and finally brought a bowl of rice. Remaining there, ignored, demonstrated his zeal for admission.

At last the aspirant was allowed to join the monks, and when winter came, the camera followed him through the harsh discipline of the *sesshin*. The first night was the only one in which the monks were allowed to lie down to sleep. For the rest of the week they slept upright on their *zafus* until the gong woke them at 3:00 a.m. to resume *zazen*.

The television screen conveyed the frozen chill of the *zendo* through the breath of the meditators visible in the unheated room and glimpses of snow outside the rice paper walls. This chill, the meager meals of rice and tea, and the long hours of sitting made our own retreat look like a luxury vacation. There were no massages for these monks.

The rigor reminded me of the self-flagellation and hair shirts of medieval Christian hermits, but Father Hand stressed that mortification of the flesh is not the purpose. Zen discipline is designed to wake up the monks the way Riley's cousin was awakened in the barn. Once I heard a Zen priest say that the training was meant to break you to the point where you could no longer maintain a facade of control. With little sleep and the strain of sitting still for long periods, the weakened ego had to cry uncle and give up its dominance.

Evelyn Underhill sheds some light on the necessity for such measures in *Mysticism,* where she writes, "This strange art of contemplation...demands of the self which undertakes it the same hard dull work, the same slow training of the will which lies behind all supreme achievement and is the price of all true liberty. It is the want of such training...which is responsible for the mass of vague, ineffectual, and sometimes harmful mysticism...the dilute cosmic emotion and limp spirituality which hang...on the skirts of the true seekers of the Absolute."

The message was clear: no dabblers allowed, no "dilute cosmic emotion." The striking of the wood announced matters of life and death like a rifle shot. Get to work. Breathe in. Breathe out. No fidgeting, no slouching, no castle-building.

"Maintain mindfulness," Father Hand directed us as we rose for walking. "Do not let yourself be distracted. *Kinhin* was not a break but a continuation of the concentration we had been pursuing. There were to be no breaks, no escape from the present moment.

Outside of the Rose Room, too, every act, every movement was to be done with attention. Putting on shoes, opening a door, taking a shower—no precious second was to pass unnoticed. Forget the past and future. Forget trying to be someone you're not. Forget your illusions. Look and see what is under your nose. I was astounded at the effort it took.

The absence of conversation at meals helped. I noticed how conversation usually usurps my awareness of what and how much I am eating. Even at those times when I eat at home alone, I'll turn on the television news or read rather than give my full attention to the food in front of me. At the retreat I breathed in the aroma of the vegetable soup before I took my first spoonful and tasted individual grains of rice. I began to perceive the amount of food that leaves me satisfied.

Facing each other for meals at round tables seating five or six produced some initial awkwardness. But tapes of Gregorian chants or Native American flute music smoothed over any embarrassment, and by dinner that day it seemed natural to eat without talking. Linda and Richard both told me after the retreat that they were relieved at not having to make conversation. I felt relief, too, but also curiosity about how the others were faring. It was just as well I couldn't ask them then, since the inevitable comparisons that resulted from such discussion would only have worsened my negative self-evaluation.

Geoff placed on the table a book that he carried with him, Thic Nhat Hanh's *The Miracle of Mindfulness*, the kind of book that emphasizes practice rather than theory and fit Father Hand's description of a book that could be read in brief segments for inspiration. Nhat Hanh relates in it how he observes his friend eat a tangerine without paying attention to what he was doing. He remarks, "It was as if he hadn't been eating the tangerine at all. If he had been eating anything, he was 'eating' his future plans." I too had been "eating" mostly the past and future and now I was beginning to learn to eat my soup and my rice instead.

After dinner I navigated my way through the labyrinthine hallways to a door that led outside. The summer sun lit up the tips of the foliage on the oak trees as if they were hundreds of green candles. I walked briskly on the pathways circling the grounds passing and nodding to Peter, who sat to my right in the Rose Room. My leg muscles needed the stretch and I breathed deeply of the warm air.

When I stopped at my room before the evening meeting, I found a bouquet of flowers in front of my door, another mistake, I assumed, like the message for Linda. My name, however, was on the card and inside was the signature of my husband with wishes for a good retreat. I arranged the summer mixture of apricot, violet, and golden blooms on my desktop. The eruption of color transformed the bare little room and I sat on my bed, wonderstruck by this unexpected gift. Receiving the flowers touched me so deeply, I suspected, because they were completely unanticipated and came in the midst of growing discouragement. They reminded me of the possibility of undeserved and unlooked for grace.

In fact, the cheer brought by the flowers made me realize how dejected I had become in the last two days from watching the trivial and self-seeking contents of my own mind. I couldn't comprehend how such dismal revelations about myself could possibly foster self-acceptance. "The gruesome part of sitting...is to begin to see what is really going on in our mind," states Charlotte Joko Beck in *Everyday Zen.* "It is a shocker for all of us."

Most everyone I talked to after the retreat reported discomfort at the relentless hours of facing their own thoughts.

For Geoff, the silence intensified the pain of uncertainty about his career direction. Clare saw how much anxiety she had about becoming ill and dependent on others in old age. For Marianne, memories of painful experiences would arise with full emotional impact. She maintained, "I think if anybody just got quiet enough, the crap would begin coming up."

The temptation to censor the unpleasant with daydreams was overwhelming. True self-acceptance required disillusionment about who we thought ourselves to be. Without the distraction of conversation, we had little choice but to become accustomed to what we saw.

In the evening, walking with the candles flickering, our shadows crossed and mingled on the Rose Room walls, where we looked like dancers in some cosmic ritual. One of our chants came to my mind. "Dance in the darkness, slow be the pace. Surrender to the rhythm of redeeming grace." Were disillusionment and discouragement the rhythm of grace? Was this a dance of sleepwalkers trying to wake up?

Foreboding about the rest of the week, about the fog, came over me as I put one foot in front of the other. With each step I could feel the soreness in my knees. My anticipating mind imagined physical and mental trials ahead — maybe not as extreme as for the Japanese Zen Buddhists but enough to hurt. As we filed out of the Rose Room, Father Hand reminded us that we would begin the more intensive schedule the next day, which meant an earlier start.

I climbed the stairs anticipating and rehearsing the week to come. Lying awake in bed, I replayed and re-created scenes from more comfortable vacations spent at the beach or in the mountains. The dance of the past and the future went on and on. Somewhere in the midst of it was what I was looking for: the still point of the turning world.

4. Day Four: Falling Apart

When the grizzly lunged at me with teeth bared, I woke up, shaking. The sight of the clock glowing 2 a.m. assured me that this had been a bad dream, but it was the kind of nightmare that floods the waking mind. Engulfed in fresh terror I lay stark still, trying to breathe. The trembling of my body and the pounding of my heart gave way to a tightness in my chest, stomach pains, and a growing sensation of nausea.

Afraid to move but convinced that I was going to be sick, I forced myself out of bed for the trek down the hall to the bathroom. At the door, I heard a creak in the corridor and froze, certain that an axe murderer was loose in the building. After standing motionless for long minutes in the pitch blackness while the queasiness in my stomach and the pains in my chest worsened, I grabbed the chain lock to unhitch it. It wouldn't budge. Frantically I jiggled the knob but nothing would move. I thought I remembered that the symptoms of a heart attack sometimes included nausea along with pains in the chest.

Sweating, I found the light switch and turned it on, blinking in the brightness. It looked like I had inserted the end of the chain in the wrong hole, locking myself in. I was trapped. Fighting back panic, I deliberated whether to bang on the walls and call for help then or wait until I heard people stirring.

I glared at the lock. Finally, I saw that the knob I had been trying to remove was the one on the stationary end of the chain. The other end came out easily. The hallway was empty and in the bathroom my nausea disappeared. I collapsed back into bed with relief that I hadn't wakened my neighbors.

In the daylight it was clear that I had suffered a panic attack over my dread of the more rigorous schedule. I couldn't imagine surviving a day of increased sitting, much less the rest of the week. By this time, my body was a wreck. All my muscles and joints hurt, and the pain was as much from tension as from keeping my legs folded for hours. My neck was so stiff I could barely turn it, and knots clutching my back and shoulders made sitting upright an ordeal. Later I read a comment by Mark Epstein and Jonathan Lieff in *Transformations of Consciousness* that described what was happening to me. Straining too hard to achieve a state of concentration, they explain, "can cause a paradoxical increase in anxiety and mental agitation, associated with such physical symptoms as upper back and neck pain."

Anxiety and agitation had replaced the torpor of the previous morning. The silence was acting as an abrasive, peeling away the layers of the persona I considered to be myself. I clung to those protective layers with growing fear. My whole being was resisting whatever I might find underneath.

I tried to follow Chiao-Lin's advice about using pain to stay in the here and now, but the pain and fear of the present were exactly what I wanted to escape. The problem was that the physical pain couldn't be ignored, and my nightmare showed that I couldn't escape the fear either. I was trapped, as I thought I had been in my room.

On the way to breakfast I ran my hand through my hair trying to remember if I'd combed it that morning. Suddenly my rumpled sweats made me feel horribly disheveled. Looking around my table, I was amazed at how well-groomed and neatly dressed everyone looked. I took a bite of oatmeal. Here I was, even in my distress, worrying about my appearance and judging myself negatively in comparison to others. There seemed to be no way out of these thought patterns.

The new schedule called for meditation after breakfast in place of the morning talk. I folded a towel under my *zafu* in an attempt to find some relief for my legs. I noticed others making adjustments as well. Pillows appeared on chair backs; *zafus* were traded for prayer benches.

Instead of the usual musings on the past and future, a vivid picture of my own face appeared in my mind. I watched it as if I were looking in a mirror, and the face began to change. The wrinkles deepened, the jowls sagged, and the hair turned white. Then, as I stared in horrified stupefaction, my eyes receded into their sockets and my flesh shriveled. The grisly transmogrification didn't stop until the skin had all fallen away and I gaped at my own skeleton.

When the gong rang out the end of that session, I burst outside gasping for air. Inhaling deeply of the chill, damp fog, I headed up an acacia-lined path carpeted with the trees' dried pods and leaves. Knowing that I was going to die someday was an altogether different matter from watching my death and decay take place in front of my eyes. This graphic vision of my own demise left me more shaken than the nightmare of the bear attack. I strode briskly, feeling the life pulsing through my veins.

In a grassy clearing I stopped and collapsed on the ground, flattening my back against the earth. I craved the warmth of the sun beginning to break through the fog. Treetops framed a circle of emerging sky. In the center of the circle a yellow leaf spiralled in slow motion through the air and landed on my chest. A hawk dipped through the shreds of fog. It occurred to me that the tree the leaf came from and the hawk would crumple to the ground one day just as I saw myself die. We'd all eventually make compost for the earth.

It was time for either mass or another meditation session before lunch, but my body did not possess the energy required to move. The sun had vanquished the fog. Stretching out in its warmth soothed my aching bones. Depleted physically and emotionally, I could no longer fend off the truths that were becoming evident in the stillness. I did live almost completely in the past and future. I did judge myself constantly and compare my performance to that of others. My body was aging and would die.

Chiao-Lin's words came back to me that it is not so much pain that causes suffering but rather the avoidance of pain. At home I avoided such painful truths with continual activity. On the retreat my mind was creating all kinds of distractions. Now at last these avoidance mechanisms were unraveling. My defenses were becoming exhausted.

I heard footsteps on the path and saw myself as the passerby would, sprawled out like a victim of a train wreck. My will to keep up a good front had vanished. There was liberation in hitting bottom. I had failed the course, was immobilized, and anyone could come and gawk for all I cared. I fell asleep in the sun.

When I woke up I was hungry and shuffled to the dining room, emptied by then of the lunch crowd. Scrounging up a cold grilled cheese sandwich and an apple, I took my finds back outside to eat on a bench in the comforting sunshine. I remembered the words from an audio tape Father Hand had played by James Finley, a former student of Thomas Merton and currently a psychiatrist. Finley stated that the crisis precipitated by monastic life is that you realize you're not going to make it. In that crisis, he said, you discover that the real object of counting breaths is not to get to ten but to learn to return to one, over and over again.

It was a crushing blow to my ego to admit that I couldn't carry out the simple acts of sitting on a cushion and counting ten consecutive breaths without distraction. With my hopes for achieving even this abandoned, I no longer had anything to gain and therefore, as Finley put it, nothing to lose.

At the afternoon talk, Father Hand continued with the prologue to the gospel of John. He read, "The light shines on in the darkness, a darkness that did not overcome it." "Before we can find the light," he declared, "we have to honestly admit our darkness." This darkness he defined as being stuck in ego-centered consciousness.

In my current state, admitting my darkness was not difficult to do. "Stuck" described precisely how I felt. I was stuck at one, stuck in the self-criticism that produced anxiety and depression, and I couldn't make the changes necessary to function any differently. The only further change I could imagine more sitting producing in me was a permanent inability to walk.

"Instead of identifying with our bodies and with what we do," Father Hand continued, "we have to find our true identity in the infinite." His first Zen master, Yasutani Hakuun Roshi put it this way: "First you must get rid of the *ji-ga*, or individual ego, then you must get rid of the *ia-no-ga* or family ego, then goes the *kuni-no-ga* or national ego, and finally the *shyukyo-no-ga* or religious ego. Our ultimate identity is not in our ego, our family, our country, or our religion. When we discover this, we truly become children of God."

Father Hand then read us a story written by a woman who was sixteen when her eighteen-year-old brother was killed in an accident. They had been very close, and she became despondent at his death. For four years she anguished over the question of why we are given life only to have it taken away. The answer came to her unbidden one night as she was falling asleep. It was not an explanation but an overwhelming sense of inner peace and joy in being part of existence.

Several years later her experience had faded. It was then that she learned about the discipline of meditation through which she rediscovered the peace and joy she had known and lost. At a Zen *sesshin* she experienced the *satori* that convinced her, "No matter what happens in the world, it will somehow be all right....I feel so free," she said, "to really live, to just be."

Her conclusion reminded me of Julian of Norwich's saying, which we chanted the day before at the closing of mass: "All shall be well, and all shall be well, and all manner of things shall be well." Rachel Hosmer writes in *Gender and God* that this phrase is often quoted "with little understanding of what soul-searching anguish it cost Julian to maintain it." It seemed that darkness was the price that had to be paid for lasting joy.

At the end of the talk Marianne asked Father Hand if all enlightenment experiences happen suddenly, like this woman's. He replied that a gradual awakening is much more common. Most of the people he's observed tend to take two steps forward and then a step back rather than have one momentous experience that never fades. He added that these forward leaps rarely happen during meditation, which prepares the way for changes that often come later.

This comment gave me one more reason to let go of any expectations. It was clear that the experience of the woman Father Hand told about stemmed from a suffering I had no desire to duplicate. My own wretched state had reduced my hopes for the week to mere survival.

When the group moved across the hall, I lagged behind, unable to imagine enduring another round of sitting. My eyes met Marianne's and her look told me that she too was having a rough time. I followed her reluctantly into the Rose Room, sustained by our shared misery.

I eyed my *zafu* warily, as if it were an instrument of torture, then sat down on it, hugging my knees to my chest. Peter, on my right, sat in a kneeling position on his low bench. Not once had he made a detectable motion or sound during meditation. In the facing row, Felicite beamed from her arrangement of pillows. I rested my forehead on my bent knees, unwilling to move into a position that caused so much pain.

All the chairs were taken, and I lacked the energy to dig up another one and fit it into the already full back rows that held the chairs. Also, I found that I had developed some kind of perverse attachment to my cushion that kept me rooted to it. I had already tried alternating my cross-legged, or quarter-lotus, position with a kneeling, or *seiza*, position supported by the *zafu* on its side. When the vibrations of the final gong faded I was convinced that there was nothing else to be done but raise my head, position my legs, and take a deep breath.

"The opportunity to experience real silence occurs when we have been driven into a corner and simply cannot move an inch," writes the Zen teacher Dainin Katagiri in *Returning to Silence*. Something had changed in the nature of the silence that had nothing to do with the presence or absence of noise inside or outside of the room. Maybe it was the silence of knowing I had nowhere else to go but into whatever I was avoiding in the present. I breathed out. One. I breathed in and exhaled again. Two. The silence took hold of me and carried me into its center. I felt myself losing my bearings. All I could sense was a deep, dark, bottomless abyss in front of me, waiting to swallow me up. I teetered precariously on the edge.

The one thing that was clear to me was that falling into that black hole meant annihilation. I clung to my breathing for dear life while the maw grew. All the muscles in my body clenched, increasing my pain. This fear reached beyond the panic of the night before. I could no longer escape into the past or the present. All that filled my awareness was this gaping void that threatened my very existence.

Chiao-Lin's voice broke in with the commanding words, "You must surrender." Surely she didn't mean to the abyss. She had to be crazy to suggest surrendering voluntarily. I was determined to cling to the edge and fight annihilation.

Walking between meditation periods, I could reflect enough to entertain the notion that I might be coming mentally unglued. Afterward, several people told me that they experienced some kind of disintegration of the control they maintained in their daily lives. Felicite's experience was the most similar to my own. She related that when she began meditating four years before, she became afraid that she would die if she surrendered to the nothingness. When the fear arose, she said, she was able to surmount it and go on meditating. During this week, however, she encountered an even stronger apprehension from which she was unable to break away.

This time she imagined herself, as I did, about to fall into an abyss. She reported, "I feared that I was going to dissolve into nothing and found myself backing away from the edge. I kept thinking that I had to warn Father Hand to call my mother and explain what had happened to me because I was certain I was going mad." Felicite said she would also find herself submerged in negative self-judgment for not being able to overcome the fear.

Clare, too, was in distress at her first meditation retreat. She told me, "I almost blew up because the silence was so horrendous. The 'monkey mind' simply would not turn off. I was afraid that something would emerge from my unconscious that would cause me to be out of control. It was frightening to see the bits and pieces of memories and thoughts about the future go through my head. I was forced to pay attention to them in a way I'd never had to do in any other circumstances."

During Clare's second week-long retreat, she had an image recur in meditation of herself crawling on coastal rocks toward a lighthouse. "I was on rough seas during those initial experiences," she revealed. "It was sheer guts that kept me going. By this retreat I had an idea of what I was in for and had built some trust in Father Hand."

For Marianne, a sense of falling apart came when she was gripped by emotions so powerful that she was unable to meditate. At these times she would be so overcome with hurt or anger or remorse over a particular memory that emerged during meditation that she would go upstairs to her room. There she would write out what she was feeling and then call her sponsor in her Twelve-Step program and read her what she had written. After these phone conversations she said, "I felt tremendous relief, as if a burden had been lifted."

Although the emotions that came up during meditation were painful to her, even at the time they occurred Marianne saw value in this process. "I've wasted much time in psychotherapy," she disclosed, "because I could talk about the emotions that were causing me problems but couldn't feel them. So I knew that when these emotions hit me in meditation I was getting a great gift."

After dinner I walked outdoors, drawn to the remaining daylight and to movement in order to escape the dark stillness that threatened to swallow me up. The sun blazed low in the sky and behind the western hills lurked a rim of fog waiting to make its nighttime entrance.

It had been a brutal day. Wakened by a panic attack, seeing myself die and rot, sitting in terror when I'd hoped to find peace—it was returning to one all right and I didn't

like it at all. A battle was going on between my instinct to
fight the fear and the voice of Chiao-Lin that said to surrender. The sense of defeat I felt made me believe that I
was losing the battle.

During the evening sitting, the fear never abated. By
forcing myself to count breaths, however, I started to
develop a cautious familiarity with the blackness. I was
like a cliff-dweller who grows accustomed to living on the
edge of the precipice.

We closed with a vespers service in which we prayed for
the hungry, the homeless, the newly born, the sick, and the
dying. We opened our hearts and our hands to all the vic-
tims of war and oppression. While we all chanted, "May
our prayers rise like incense, our hearts like an evening
sacrifice," each of us walked to the altar and burned a
pinch of incense for our own intentions.

Imagining all the suffering in the world just about did
me in. Looking out of the window in my room, I wondered
who was sick or lonely behind the house lights in the
neighborhood. My own wretchedness merged with that of
the world. I crawled under the covers conscious of those
who had no bed.

Father Hand had warned us that he would play a tape
of Korean drumming to open the next morning's meditation. He announced that if we preferred not to hear it, we
could meditate across the hall for the first session.
Accustomed to deep stillness by now, I was appalled by
the idea of such a jarring noise as drumming and considered just staying under the covers the next day. I was in
pain, exhausted, and terrified of what might happen next.
Like Felicite, I wondered if I was losing my mind. I vowed
to sign up for an individual conference with Father Hand.
Overcome by a monumental grief for my own condition
and that of all humans, I cried myself to sleep.

5. Day Five: My Eyes Are Opened

I crawled out of bed that morning defeated. My face in the mirror startled me—in four days I looked as if I had aged years. The last thing I wanted to hear was the drumming that would begin the morning session, but my capacity to resist was depleted. I followed the others into the Rose Room.

In that place where I had become so accustomed to stillness that someone's cough could make me jump, the drumbeats exploded into the morning hush like artillery fire. The insistent rhythms struck me with the force of a physical blow, magnifying the pains in my body. Convinced that any tranquility cultivated up to that point was being destroyed, I regretted not taking the option of meditating in the meeting room across the hall.

I was riveted to my cushion, though, by the pulsating din that surged into my consciousness like a tidal wave, inundating all thoughts. I lost awareness of the past and the future and of judgments about how I was doing. In my mind's eye I saw a tiny flame that grew larger and larger until I was enveloped by it. While the drums throbbed, I sat immobilized in the center of that blaze that burned away bodily pain, fear, and what was left of my resistance to the unknown. Weakened by days of struggling, I gave in and let the raging current of violent sound push me

47

over the edge of the abyss. When the last beat faded away, I was somewhere I had never been before.

This was not a trance or any other state of unreality. On the contrary, thoughts of the unreal past and future had been drummed out of my head. I had landed in a place of very deep interior silence. For the first time that week, maybe for the first time in my life, I just sat, and the sitting was truly sufficient. I was no longer waiting: for the gong to ring, for breakfast, for the end of the retreat.

When the others in the room rose for *kinhin*, I remained on my *zafu*, motionless. I heard sounds of movement, but as if from a diving bell far below a distant surface. When the last gong rang before breakfast, I was dimly conscious of everyone filing out of the room, but I sat on, anchored at the bottom of the sea of silence into which I had plummeted.

This void was more than just the absence of thoughts. It was as if I had been swallowed up in a vastness that stretched to infinity. In that voluminous silence, not a shred of fear remained. I had no idea how much time passed before I opened my eyes. When I did, the room looked strangely different, even though nothing was altered. All the colors and textures of surfaces were vibrantly electric, a palette of shimmering molecules. Instead of identifying objects, my vision focused on details such as grain in the wood and patterns of light. In this way familiar surroundings metamorphosed into the extraordinary.

It occurred to me to stand up, but my body seemed to be stuck where it was. Some link was missing in the chain of command, and I was unable to translate the thought of standing up into action. What had been automatic before suddenly seemed like an extremely complicated procedure that I once knew and had forgotten. I had to invent a method for standing up all over again from scratch.

Overtaken with minutiae, I maneuvered my body into an upright position one movement at a time.

I was so locked into the present moment that I had lost the memory of how to move. I felt shaky though and thought of getting something to eat in the same way I might think of feeding my cat or watering a plant. With my capacity for anticipating and rehearsing gone, I had no ability to plan for the future. The project of conveying myself up a flight of stairs to the dining room seemed as remote and inconceivable as a mission to Venus. My entire being was becalmed in the stillness of the present.

I piloted myself in the same way I had stood up: by devising each motion required step-by-step. My body resisted all movement, however, and frequently just came to a halt. Without momentum, it took a prodigious effort to reach the dining room.

Clare, Geoff, and a couple of others lingered there, sipping coffee and listening to the music still playing. With great effort I placed some juice and cereal in front of me on a table, then found that I had no appetite. To quell the shakiness though, I forced myself to sip some juice, and as I did tears started to roll down my face. I had no idea why I was crying. Something inside of me seemed to have broken loose. I sat until the weeping subsided, then propelled myself outdoors.

I had walked out the same door many times that week, but this time everything seemed transformed, as if I had landed on another planet. I stood marvelling at the sensation of moist fog particles touching my skin. I inhaled the pungent eucalyptus fragrance that I hadn't noticed in the air before. A row of those giant trees loomed in front of me, their smooth, rosy flesh exposed by great swags of peeling bark. I stood before them transfixed at what I had passed so many times and never really seen.

Among the eucalyptus trees I began navigating more

easily by bypassing the conscious mental process altogether. All sense of time had disappeared. When the fog began to dissolve in the sun, I found myself heading toward the grassy clearing where I had collapsed the day before. I followed the trail through the clearing into the wood of oaks and bay trees. There, sunshine filtered through the archway of branches and dappled the path like light pouring through a stained glass window.

I sat down on a wooden bench next to the creek and listened to the trickling water. A glossy blackberry dangled from its thorny foliage in front of me, plump with juice. I picked the berry and held it in my palm, dazzled by its ripe perfection. When I put it in my mouth, the lush nectar spurted over my tongue and washed my senses with its sweetness. I basked in the filtered light, engulfed by the taste of the berry, the scent of bay, and the sound of the rippling creekwater.

After awhile I found myself moving in the direction of the Rose Room. I joined the group during a break for *kinhin* and sat with gratitude and equanimity for the rest of the morning. At lunch I ate only a little soup. My gluttonous preoccupation with food had mutated into a loss of appetite.

When I took my bowl into the area of the kitchen designated for scraping and stacking, I noticed none of my usual tendency to hurry through the chores. No longer thinking about what I was going to do next, I became totally absorbed in the task at hand. I was as content to be present with the garbage and the dirty dishes in the same way I had been present in the woods by the creek.

This loss of discrimination between the desirable and undesirable manifested itself again later in the day when I passed an asphalt machine on a back road of the retreat grounds. It was belching the stench of tar, a smell to which I'd always had an aversion. For once, I didn't hold my nose and hurry by. The road needed repair and it seemed to me cause for gratitude that such a machine was there to do the job.

I no longer flinched at the sight of my *zafu*. When I sat, I sat; when I walked, I walked. What had been so arduous suddenly seemed easy. The aches in my neck, back and legs had returned but no longer dominated my attention. Thoughts drifted in and out of my awareness without the hold on me they had previously commanded. External disturbances like a cough or kitchen noises all merged with the nameless immensity I had become a part of.

One phrase recurred in my mind throughout the day: "I am the singular, unique incarnation of the glory of God." This was no longer a notion subject to speculation by the intellect but an irrefutable reality. The persistent thoughts of past and future had subsided, and in the still point of the present I could accept myself as complete. I was no longer becoming but was content to be.

Wheeling around a hallway corner on my way from outdoors to the Rose Room, I met Chiao-Lin, and in her eyes I could see reflected my own exhilaration. My rumpled clothes and frizzed hair hadn't changed from the previous day when I perceived myself as unkempt, but on this day I felt myself glowing with an inner radiance that Chiao-Lin beamed back at me.

At the afternoon talk one of the Sisters asked what meditation has to do with love. Father Hand responded that we look for commonality with others as signs of love. If we like the same music or have the same opinions about politics or religion, we think we have a basis for love. But the only true commonality is that we are all manifestations of the same Source. Finding that commonality through meditation is the basis for genuine love.

When I stretched out beneath an oak tree with grass blades cooling the bare skin of my face, arms and feet, I felt that commonality with the bug staggering across my arm. Passing Ada on the stairway, I pressed my palms together and made a bow to her in recognition of the Source in her. In the meeting room I looked around and saw a manifestation of the infinite in every face. The differences between us that had once made me anxious seemed as natural as the differences between an oak and a eucalyptus tree.

At the time I had no capacity or inclination to interpret what was happening, but I knew later that this was not an enlightenment experience in which I saw myself as one with the universe. It was, rather, a glimpse of a reality I had been shut out from entirely, the two steps forward of which Father Hand had spoken. The transformation was such a dramatic one because I had been so asleep, so mired in self-consciousness that any shift in my perspective at all would seem monumental.

Two factors made this shift possible. The first was seeing my desire for the approval of others exposed in the retreat setting as futile. Without objectives, there was nothing to achieve (aside from showing up). The old rules had been discarded and so my judgments based on the old rules had to go as well.

This insight was reflected in the phrase that recurred so frequently in my mind, "I am the unique incarnation of the glory of God." The Zen teacher Daiun Harada-roshi, quoted in Philip Kapleau's *The Three Pillars of Zen*, makes a similar statement in defining the experience of seeing into one's true nature called "kensho." He says, "It is the sudden realization that 'I have been complete and perfect from the very beginning. How wonderful, how miraculous'!"

The second critical element was embracing my misery instead of fighting it. Once I had been rendered incapable of resisting the flood of fear and pain, I could surrender my control, as Chiao-Lin had so often told us to do. The tears I cried myself to sleep with the night before exposed my "shoulds" as futile and neurotic attempts at perfectionism. My idealistic pretenses had been demolished by the truths exposed in the silence.

Ken Wilber writes in *No Boundary* that at the "very point where absolutely everything seems wrong, everything spontaneously becomes right." To embrace inner reality, no matter how appalling, is to give up trying to change it. That is true acceptance, and with it comes the flood of joy.

Several people I spoke to after the retreat mentioned experiences with the impact of the one I'd had. They all attested to difficulty in describing these experiences. Felicite recalled the great joy she encountered in attention to the present moment. She observed, "When I was able to experience directly, without the constant censoring I usually do, then I felt freed up, energetic, joyful. I kept thinking, Wouldn't it be wonderful to live like this?"

Linda reported that for her the peak experiences of the retreat came through the liturgy as well as meditating on the rosary and scripture. She said, "I would stay with a line of the rosary for an hour. Its mysteries are very deep for me; I'm always given a gift if I meditate on them or on the words of the Bible. I accept what I get and it's not up for debate." At times during the retreat, she disclosed, "I felt a pulsating, heart throbbing life force giving something to me. This was the power of the Spirit."

Clare described a powerful experience of knowing that her breath went all the way back to the "big bang." She related, "This made me feel that I was connected to all that has gone before. I came to know that I have a fundamental relationship to the planet and to every living thing."

After this, she found herself living more in the present and dwelling less on fears for the future or memories from the past. She commented, "I realized that I couldn't change the past and I could do a relatively small amount of planning for the future. So essentially I was stuck in the present and I had better be there. When I saw this, I could settle into just sitting. It was as simple and profound as that." She added that she also lost her fear of the unconscious. "Whatever emerges," she said, "I now look at it as something I can use. I see it as creative."

In the talk that afternoon, Father Hand told us the story of Ignatius of Loyola, the sixteenth-century Spanish nobleman who founded the order of the Jesuits. Ignatius was a scholar who also had many religious visions in his life. He concluded, however, that the experience which taught him more than all his studies and visions combined occurred one morning along the bank of a river. He couldn't describe what happened except to say afterward that he could "see God in all things."

This was what we were here for; we wanted nothing less than to see God. That night before I turned off the light I tried to write about the quest. I gave the poem the name of the path by the creek:

Water Way

Seeking what Ignatius found at his stream,
Pilgrims follow this path in processional,
Passing the stations of cypress and oak,
Entering the chapel of dappled light,
Breathing the incense of bay.

Blackberry on a thorn-crowned altar,
Ripe consecrated offering,
Stains lips with the crimson juice
Of a celestial celebration.
The seekers are found.

6. Day Six: In the Flow

Even before my alarm sounded, I woke up rested. Getting out of bed, walking downstairs, stretching, bowing, and sitting all came effortlessly. Instead of deliberating over every move, I just moved. It was as if I'd been dragging around chains that had suddenly fallen off.

In the dim morning light of the Rose Room Father Hand spoke a line from the Psalm:

"Be still and know I am God."

"Then he said, "Be still and know I am."

"Be still."

"Be."

This was the simplification going on in meditation: a movement from the effort to be still and the effort to know toward effortless being. It was a movement from the concept of God to the experience of God. Without this duality between concept and experience, the struggle ceased. There was nothing to attain.

At mid-morning, I was passing a cluster of people waiting for the elevator when a sturdy, grey-haired woman approached the group and asked for the person who had the massage appointment. Here was the Sister who gave massages, standing right in front of me! I seized my chance. When she agreed to work me into her schedule, I beamed with glee. Just the thought of a massage made my muscles feel better.

I was astonished at the ease of arranging what had previously seemed impossibly complicated. It revealed some flow to existence that I had joined once my grasp on control relaxed. Had I been hindering my own cooperation with the beneficence of the universe? Or had I just been blinded to the existing flow because I was too busy trying to carry out my own agenda?

What had changed in my way of operating was that I'd given up trying to make something happen. I had arrived at an inner conviction that I needed nothing more, internally or externally, than what I had. I had stopped excavating events from the past or striving toward goals in the future. No longer compelled to escape or manipulate the present, I could reap its bounty.

When I stretched out on the massage table, it was the wreckage of the week's battle with control lying there. Sister Leona said a prayer, turned on a tape of classical guitar music, and began with my neck. Her strong hands found and kneaded the knots into submission, then moved on to my back and legs. When the massage was over, I was too limp to move. Mercifully, she left my body, shrouded with a sheet, to revive at its own pace.

The massage did not eradicate all pain but softened it considerably. My legs continued to hurt, an inevitable side-effect of sitting for so many hours in a cross-legged position. Some soreness in my neck, back, and shoulders remained as well, but this was alleviated by a loss of the tension that caused it.

After lunch I followed a path through an oak grove. A towhee perched on a branch close enough to touch didn't fly away when I passed. I walked on the earth so softly that I didn't even scare the birds. On a higher branch of another tree I caught sight of a blue jay jabbing at nits under its wing. Such an awkward, intimate gesture so unlike the jay's usual cocky self-assurance made me feel as if I'd peeked into a private world. Could it be possible that I had passed by such spectacles before, too preoccupied to notice?

Attuned to the marvels around me, I was flooded with sensation at every step. The patterns of light and shade under the trees, the crackle of dry oak leaves beneath my feet were so vividly acute that I ached to hold on to each sight and sound. One impression would dissolve into the next, forcing me to let go of each wonder. None of it would hold still for me to grasp, so that the transcendent joy of each breathtaking moment was accompanied by the wrenching sorrow of loss. This was not an intellectual understanding of the transitory nature of life but an experience of the death of every passing second. Each wondrous breath of air and ray of sunlight had to be given up. The truth penetrated to my core that I had absolutely nothing to hold on to.

I sank onto a low branch of an oak and rested my back against the trunk. This week I had seen that the past and future were illusory. I had visualized my own death and decay. And I had begun to accept all this. But colliding with the impermanence of the present was more than I could stand. Already attachment to my newfound awareness was causing me pain.

After the retreat I found an explanation of what was happening spelled out by Joseph Goldstein in *Speaking of Silence*. He states, "As we pay careful attention to the process of mind and body, we begin to experience that what we are *is* the unfolding of momentary experience — moments of seeing, hearing, tasting, smelling, touching, thinking, mind states....We *are* this changing process." Through this kind of awareness "we gradually begin to let go of our attachment to the particular constellation of experience we call 'self.' " What had seemed like giving up a succession of external experiences was actually a step toward giving up the self having the experience. This is why it felt like dying.

The day's talk addressed what it means to give up the self. Speaking about the work of Ken Wilber on the evolution of consciousness, Father Hand observed that the stages Wilber describes represent the human spiritual path. Most adults are in the mental-ego state, which is dominated by self-consciousness. Once in a while we break through this ego domination into a heightened awareness. Most of us inevitably regress, but after such an experience we live with a knowledge of what is possible. To me, breaking through felt like the anesthetic had worn off and I had just woken up. I was beginning to feel again: both joy and pain.

After the talk, Geoff questioned the wisdom of giving up the ego when most adults are still in the process of finding and developing this sense of self. Father Hand answered that our aim is not to lose the ego, which is necessary for our functioning in the world, but to transcend it by expanding the reality we identify with beyond this narrow concept of self. Putting the ego to death, Father Hand told Geoff, means that we no longer allow this narrow perspective to dominate us.

Psychologists stress the development of the ego. The religious stress the process of losing the ego. Both are correct. A firm sense of one's individual identity as well as a growing sense of one's infinite identity are both essential components to psychological and spiritual health.

During the intensive meditation of the retreat, however, my ego felt itself threatened. The abyss that menaced me so frighteningly represented the leap beyond who I thought myself to be. A sensation of dying with the passing of each moment revealed how reluctant I was to give up my idea of a fixed core self for the reality of continual permutation. The glimmer I'd experienced of my world in flux made me feel as if I were on a carnival ride. The perpetual motion was making me dizzy. Since clinging to the idea of a fixed self caused me grief, however, I had to wonder whether it was my own suffering that I didn't want to give up.

In the Rose Room we chanted,

> O Great Spirit
> Earth, sun, sky, and sea:
> You are inside
> And all around me.

The earth had rotated our portion of the world into late afternoon. In that room I took more notice than usual of the particular character and mood of each time of day. Sitting in the early morning was a different experience from sitting when the sun was high in the sky. I was different.

I was becoming aware of the dance of the earth and sun that must be deeply imprinted in the human psyche. The Rose Room's high windows overlooked a courtyard walled in on all sides by the building. Yet it was inside this enclosure more than anywhere else that I detected the ever-shifting cycles of the earth.

This kind of awareness loosened the shackles of self-consciousness. With my grip on the small, limited self slackened, I could see my place in the cycles of earth and sun, birth and death. And I felt, more than I ever had in my entire life, that it was completely all right to be me.

Outdoors after dinner, the squirrel show was in progress. One of these chattering creatures lunged down a tree trunk, spotted me, then scuttled back up. After many such sprints, he landed on the ground, but his scolding and nervous glances in my direction told me that he couldn't bring himself to bury his acorn while I watched. I had to laugh. His nervous flurry reminded me of my usual frantic bustle, always looking over my shoulder to see who was looking. All this commotion was based on a belief that accumulating the human equivalent of acorns was what gave me worth.

I stretched out on the grass and basked in the golden wash from the sinking sun. A towhee, maybe the one I passed so closely that morning, hopped and chirped beside me, pecking at invisible morsels. Engrossed in every flick of that bird's feather and every bob of the head, I forgot the moments passing.

Paradoxically, contracting the attention down to one simple focus, as we were doing in meditation, results in an expansion of awareness. My absorption in a bird or a squirrel — as with the drumming and the breath — allowed enough forgetfulness of self to create a gap into which a larger reality could flow. This reality colored everything I saw just like the glow from the sun.

Clearly, I was not losing a self but finding one, the true self. What had begun to drop away was the self full of anxieties, insecurities, and resentments, the self-conscious ego living entirely in the past and the future. Is this what I'd been so afraid to lose?

In *Being in Love*, William Johnston relates Thomas Merton's conviction that putting the ego in the center of things creates a distorted picture of reality. According to Johnston, Merton said in his last lecture before his death that Christianity and Buddhism agree that "this experience of ourselves as absolutely autonomous individual egos is the source of all our problems." I could begin to let go of my attachment to this ego self only because it had become apparent how many problems in my life clinging to the ego had created for me.

Having unclasped my ego self enough to expand my awareness, however, I then wanted to clasp the very experience of awareness. Teachers of both East and West warn of attachment to unusual experiences as an obstacle to spiritual progress. It is human nature to prefer joy and want to preserve it, but it must be let go along with suffering.

When I spoke to Ada after the retreat she told me about what she called "big experiences." When she related these to a Buddhist teacher, however, he said, "They are nothing. You must not pay attention to experiences." She said that when she heard this she was hurt, even devastated. But she came to see that it was true and that letting everything go is essential to accepting the ephemeral nature of the universe.

Thomas Keating expresses a similar view in the Christian perspective on meditation experiences. He writes in *Open Mind, Open Heart*, "I am convinced that it is a mistake to identify the *experience* of contemplative prayer with contemplative prayer itself, which transcends any impression of God's radiating or inflowing presence.... Pure faith, according to John of the Cross, is a ray of darkness to the soul. There is no faculty that can perceive it.... One can only remark its presence by its fruits in one's life."

After the closing prayers of the evening session, most of the group filed out of the room, and I sat on in the quiet with Ada, Geoff, and a few others. The candles flickered and the incense burned out. The room was empty of audible breathing or motion but charged with the presence of those who had been emptying themselves in that place. I was buoyed by the potent hush and didn't want to leave. The next day was the last full day of the retreat, and I had developed an attachment to the very place I once wondered whether I could endure!

Everyone was gone when I left the Rose Room. The lights had been turned off in the hallway and on the stairs. When I reached the fourth floor, instead of turning into the hall leading to my room, I continued up the stairway and through a doorway to the roof. Stepping across the flat asphalt surface to the wall at the edge, I could see a thick layer of fog hugging the ground, held down in an inversion by a layer of warm air. City lights above the fog glimmered brightly against the dark mountain. Noises were amplified by the inversion.

The clarity of the lights and the sonorous rumble of jets and freeway traffic gave the scene a sparkling vibrancy. I breathed in the warmth, and my desire to cling to this night hit me with full force. I wanted to wake up all the others and bring them up to that magical scene.

On the first day of the retreat, Chiao-Lin opened one session by saying, "There is nothing to worry about." She meant for us to set aside our problems and conflicts for the week because they didn't threaten us here. That night I saw a different meaning in her words. In a real, ultimate sense, there *was* nothing to worry about. Being in the flow meant that everything happened just as it was meant to happen, although on the level of worldly concerns, this could be argued.

But there was another level, which I had come upon this week, in which this was true. It was clear in the view from the roof or in the movement of a bird. It could be found in a place not touched by the world of jet planes and freeway traffic: a place of stillness and silence. I stood on the roof gazing into that world until I could stand no more.

7. Day Seven: Departure

On the last full day of the retreat, an exuberant silence filled the air. We'd lived! In the lunch line I squinted at unidentifiable white shapes in a salad bowl; then my eyes met Ada's and we broke into muffled snickers over another of the kitchen's mystery dishes. Whispers erupted here and there throughout the day, and Father Hand reminded us that the retreat wasn't over. Chiao-Lin announced that the last day was the time to make an extra effort and increase our concentration. But a festive conviviality was in the air — and relief. Together we had made the climb and circled the mountain.

Getting up from my cushion after one meditation period, I caught a glimpse of Geoff out of the corner of my eye. He wasn't standing up in the usual way but bending over on all fours and pushing himself up with his hands. This time I suppressed my laughter, but his position struck me as funny because it so perfectly captured my own feeling of being pushed to my limits. Bodies as well as egos had been made to crawl here.

An atmosphere of camaraderie replaced my initial anxiety over fitting in. Coming face-to-face hour after hour with inner reality diminished the power of the surface self, the part of me that's concerned with how I am judged. This weakened persona resulted in a state of naked vulnerability, and the walls between me and the others collapsed.

It struck me that a kinship is formed among those walking the earth in the same place at the same time. While each of us at this particular place made our own interior journey, our presence there together contributed support and strength to our individual solitude. This happened through the heightened energy that is often present in a group but here was amplified and transformed by the silence.

As a result, I was transformed myself. Knowing this, I walked the path through the old oaks and asked myself again the question that I had pondered on the day of my arrival, "What do I seek?" I considered what I had discovered about myself this week: my dependence on the approval of others and the drive for achievement that would buy this approval. I recalled the people I'd most wanted to please in my life: parents, husband, friends, teachers, clergy, bosses. One by one, I specified what I perceived their expectations of me to be and saw what a suffocating chokehold the effort to live up to those expectations had on my life.

Then I asked myself what *I* wanted to accomplish, what signs of success would convince me that I was acceptable: a Ph.D? A Pulitzer Prize? Philanthropic works? I enumerated a list of goals from the self-indulgent to the altruistic, but could identify no one pursuit that would by itself provide ultimate fulfillment. A week of silence had tipped the balance from the desire for external rewards to the intrinsic value of being.

I passed the oak I'd sat in the day before. This was happiness: Sitting in a tree. Lying on the grass. Feeling the fog or the sunshine touching my skin. Watching a hawk circle. All ambition and seeking had fallen away. Even my desire to cling to the sensations of the moment had dissolved. I only wanted now to live my life while it was happening, not enmeshed in the past or future.

I knew the distractions of the world would come crashing back when I drove out of those gates the next day, so I considered what I could take with me as a reminder of what was important when my current state of peace was jostled and pummeled. During the day's talk Father Hand had described the many retreats he had attended in which the central activity was the making and refining of resolutions. When the retreats were over and life's demands returned with full force, he said, the resolutions always faded.

The Zen alternative to resolutions that fade is "practice." The aim is not to attain and preserve a particular state of consciousness, an impossible task anyway, but to live mindfully with full awareness of the present in every single waking moment. "Practice" is a way of life, and this is what I wanted to take with me, not new resolutions that comprised more "shoulds."

When the path I was following came to the center's upper gate, I didn't turn around but walked through it as a trial run for my departure the next day. Venturing up the narrow, winding road lined with homes tucked into the sides of the hill, I was agog at whizzing cars and chattering voices. At a bend in the road the houses on one side gave way to open space. A sign marked a trail and I turned onto it down the side of the hill, seeking refuge already even from this placid suburb. I didn't want to face the world just yet.

Instantly I was out of civilization again, in a wood of buckeyes and oaks. I chanted softly to the rhythm of my footsteps:

> Peace is flowing like a river,
> Flowing out from you and me,
> Flowing out into the desert,
> Setting all the captives free.

When I rounded a bend, the sight of a tree at a fork in the trail knocked the chant out of me. Bare of all foliage, the whitewashed trunk and branches stood starkly against the verdant surroundings. It was the tree's resemblance to a skeleton that took my breath away. Looking at it made me once again aware of the configuration of chalky bones under my flesh. In the tree, my bones seemed to be facing their likeness.

For many long minutes nothing existed but that tree and my skeleton, like sole survivors on a barren planet. It was as if the tree were reminding me not to forget the encounter with death that I had seen in my imagination. I wanted something to take with me, and now I had this indelible impression of the buckeye as a *memento mori*.

The next morning, we gathered in the meeting room after breakfast to discuss our re-entry into the world. One of the Sisters asked, "What is supposed to be the result of all this meditation in our lives?" Father Hand replied that the most important result is awareness of divine reality. He said, "You'll notice more and more that you're in the flow. It's not so much about figuring out the meaning of life as feeling the rapture of being alive."

Carol, a tall brunette and a graphics artist, raised the question of dealing with those we encounter who are habitually critical or hostile. "These people create resentment in us," Father Hand answered, "and resentment is a block to realizing our oneness with others. Seeing through the illusion of separation between us can help us deal with difficult relationships." Maybe so, but Carol's question reminded us of the individuals and situations we'd meet that were certain to shake our hard-won tranquility. It would take a great deal of practice to find detachment in the face of conflict.

We had been able to expand our ordinary states of consciousness here because such external threats to the ego that arise in daily life had been eliminated. Without the necessity of protecting the ego, we could see a reality that transcended that narrow self. The question on all of our minds was how we would respond when the threats returned.

Ken Wilber describes the fundamental shift in attitude toward others that comes with awareness that transcends the individual self. He states, "At the transpersonal level, we begin to love others not because they love us, affirm us, reflect us, or secure us in our illusions, but because they *are* us. Christ's primary teaching does not mean 'Love your neighbor as you love yourself,' but 'Love your neighbor *as* yourself.' "

Chiao-Lin and Father Hand both stressed not dissipating the energy that we had built up during the week. That precious reserve could be squandered in too much conversation or by watching too much television. Overeating or overindulgence in caffeine or alcohol would also deaden our newly found sense of aliveness, they warned.

Discipline was required, they told us, not just to meditate daily but to maintain mindfulness all of the time. This meant cultivating attention to our bodily sensations, feelings, and environment. This week of watching our inner selves would allow us to become more aware of our patterns of behavior if we didn't distract ourselves. Practicing letting go of thoughts as we did in meditation would help us not to be overwhelmed by what we saw. "Your task is to face yourself honestly," declared Chiao-Lin. "Have the courage to see what is there. Meditate every day without expectations."

We talked about how to work meditation into daily schedules. Chiao-Lin recommended choosing the time we noticed during the week when deep meditation came most easily to us. Everyone agreed that the most difficult part of meditating at home was sitting down to "do nothing" in the midst of much that needed to be done. Father Hand offered that the only resolutions that work are those that are short term and concrete: "Set a definite time for meditation and stick to it for a specified period such as a week," he suggested. "Then evaluate that time and see if it needs changing." He also told us that it helped foster the habit to meditate in the same place every day.

When we stepped into the Rose Room for the last time, the words of Shakespeare's *Henry V* sprang into my mind, "Once more into the breach, dear friends...." When Father Hand began with those very same words, I wondered if we had all tuned in to the same mental wavelength. During this last meditation session, no one moved or even breathed audibly. Or maybe I could hear no one because we breathed as one organism.

Years before, I had attended a Lenten retreat where the program included using the imagination to visualize the events leading up to the crucifixion of Jesus. At the end of the retreat, the director suggested that I continue this kind of meditation at home through the resurrection. Although my imagination had produced graphic images at the retreat, I could not conjure up a picture of the inconceivable occurrence of a resurrection. All I could do was see myself in a dark, musty tomb with a dead body and wait for something to happen. Every day I would imagine myself in that darkness, but the anticipated drama would not materialize.

Easter came and went without a resurrection. After several weeks I was about to give it up when I noticed that the picture of the tomb in my mind was subtly different from the one with which I began. A soft light allowed me to see the interior details of a cave that had become comfortably familiar. The corpse had disappeared. Some angel-like presences provided company and soft music.

All the time I thought nothing was happening — because it wasn't what I expected — the tomb had been transformed into a place of what Gregory of Nyssa calls "luminous darkness." When I tried to imagine leaving, the outside world seemed harshly bright and noisy.

Apophatic meditation, without words or images, is like sitting in the tomb. It's dark. It can be boring — or frightening. It smells of death. But that's exactly the place where the light comes on and, whether I am aware of it or not, a resurrection has occurred.

When the gong rang for the last time, we made deep bows, touching our heads to the floor in a gesture of gratitude. Then we stood and at the sound of the little bell bowed to each other and to the cross on the altar. Everyone filed out to go to the chapel for the closing mass. I stood rooted to my spot. Sunlight streamed over me through the windows, lighting up the shades of blue in the carpet and the shapes of the rocks in the sand. All week we had been learning to sit like those rocks, motionless and imperturbable. Along with the image of the buckeye, I wanted to take with me the solidity and strength of those rocks and the unshakable composure in the face of life's tumult that they signified to me.

At lunch, the dining room filled with a riotous explosion of gleeful voices, although any conversation at all seemed superfluous. Deeper connections had already been made in silence and nothing we could relate to each other seemed to capture what had gone on in this place. But the dam had broken and our ebullience overflowed.

It was too soon to talk about what had happened during the week. We all knew that its real measure would come when we returned to work and families, rude sales clerks and traffic jams. We made our good-byes swiftly. Then I was outside bidding farewell to the Iceland poppies, their parchment petals gleaming in the midday sunlight. I drove out the gates not anticipating or rehearsing what was ahead. My one thought was, "I can't believe I almost didn't do this."

Father Hand had compared meditation to listening to music. The point is in immersing oneself in the sounds, not in getting to the end. I was ready to go home, eager to see my family, but I could enjoy the process of getting there: driving a car for the first time in a week, taking in ordinary sights as if I had been out of the country for a very long time.

I tested myself by deliberately thinking about future responsibilities and upcoming events that I had worried about in meditation. The thoughts came and went and I was unable to dredge up a twinge of anxiety over them.

I had internalized the solidity of those rocks from the many hours of rocklike sitting. A firm entrenchment in the reality of the present moment shielded me from the illusions of past and future that had dominated my thinking. At the close of the final mass we had chanted, "All shall be well, and all shall be well, and all manner of things shall be well." For the first time in my life, I believed it.

8. Practice

After the retreat, I was in the flow. The air smelled fresher, foliage looked greener, food tasted better. There was a synchronicity to the events of my existence that I had never experienced before. Everything seemed to be in the right place at the right time. I was filled with tremendous joy.

I was hiking in the mountains when a small, grey fox jumped out of the brush a few yards in front of me. The animal trotted along the trail and I followed as if we were on an outing together. Then the fox popped back into a bush, leaving me convinced of my fundamental interconnection with the universe.

After several months this sense of flow was succeeded by stages resembling those of the retreat. In the three years that have passed now, these issues continue to resurface. During this time I have meditated at home daily, with a group weekly, and at occasional weekend or week-long retreats. Teachers from all traditions agree that meditation cannot have much effect unless a regular discipline is continued in this way.

I encounter the first stage in the reappearance of the question, "What do I seek?" When it is phrased, "Why am I doing this?" the question reminds me of the strength of internal and external pressure for maximum productivity. Compelling demands often appear at the time I've designated for daily meditation. When that happens, I tell myself that I will only sit for ten minutes instead of the thirty I've allotted. This works because to admit that I can't spare ten minutes in a day is to admit that I really don't want to meditate. After a few minutes on my *zafu*, the demands never seem so pressing.

"What do I seek?" is an important question to reflect on periodically, however, and as I do, the answer grows and deepens. The desire for a calm center in the midst of stress that originally sent me to that first meditation class is evolving into a longing for "the peace that passes understanding." This means that my self-centered wish for a lack of anxiety is becoming more and more a desire to live in accordance with the infinite principle of all life. The true self that I am looking for is the part of me that shares in this principle, my divine nature. Whether or not it is expressed in religious terms, this yearning of the heart reaches beyond peace of mind to a vital connection with spiritual reality that can only be experienced.

After I have reflected on my purpose, thoughts of any goal must be put aside for breathing in and breathing out: the practice of mindful attention to life in the moment. Observing the breath, the sensations of walking, and whatever it is I am doing has given me a greater sense of aliveness in the present. I'm more conscious now of the soles of my feet on the earth and the breeze touching my face. Peeling potatoes for dinner one evening while listening to Bach preludes on the stereo, I was struck with the conviction, "There is nothing else I'd rather be doing."

This surrender of my usual striving is mostly a relief. For a while, however, letting go of the pursuit of heroics produced an occasional flatness, as if I'd been running a race that had been called off. The flatness is disappearing, however, as I become accustomed to living life not as a race. In meditation, simple attention to the sensations of breathing has replaced counting my breaths, but in the sense of letting go, I am still always returning to one.

Father Hand warns that even the most disciplined practice must be guarded from becoming mechanical. There is no such thing as an experienced meditator. Every breath must be as if it is the first, every step a fresh event. This is the "beginner's mind" that Zen master Shunyru Suzuki writes about, and without it no amount of sitting can have a deep impact.

A beginner's mind leads to a sense of gratitude for everything, whether or not the desires of my ego have been granted or life is going smoothly. A grateful heart for the rushing currents as well as for the still pools puts the ego in its place. This attitude that grows out of increased awareness does not come easily in the face of difficulties, but it is worth cultivating over a lifetime.

Mindfulness practice also generates awareness of what I am resisting. When faced with unpleasant reality, I tend to manufacture distractions rather than feel discomfort, just as I did by dwelling on the past and future during the strain of sitting still for long hours. This perpetual resistance is revealed by the witness of the detached self. Over time, these observations can become discouraging. On the level of the ego, the more I see, the more frustrated I become. Yet seeing resistance to the present is the only way to overcome it. Retreats provide the opportunity to become aware of resistance in all its stark intensity. Charlotte Joko Beck describes a Zen *sesshin* as a prolonged experience of, "It's not the way I want it." At every retreat I see that I have to let go of my ego's incessant efforts to create the world in the image of my desires.

When I give in to the reality I've been resisting, I hit the bottom of the cycle where I feel as though I'm falling apart. In truth, it *is* a falling apart — of my control over the external situation as well as my own internal reaction. Sometimes this little death of the ego happens quickly; sometimes it takes weeks or months.

Bit by tiny bit, my idealized version of the way life should be is crumbling. With it, my ideal of how I should be has to go as well. As my reliance on the approval of others diminishes, I am able to accept aspects of myself that I could never acknowledge before.

The contemplative traditions of both East and West describe a process of purgation that follows an initial awakening experience. This integration of expanded awareness into everyday life is always portrayed as a struggle. Evelyn Underhill defines the purgation of Christian mystics as "a process of getting rid of all those elements of normal experience which are not in harmony with reality."

In the Zen tradition, the "Oxherding Pictures" that illustrate phases of spiritual development also depict something like purgation. The initial awakening experience or "first glimpse of the ox" must be followed by self-discipline in order to preserve the insight of the original experience and allow the resulting changes to take root. Moving toward the awakening of "catching the ox" demands a purgation of illusions — everything "not in harmony with reality" must be let go. In both the Zen and Christian traditions this work demands suffering, not for its own sake, but as a means to greater freedom. Such discipline is not deprivation but an acknowledgment that any change needs reinforcing in order to become part of one's life.

The acts of austerity traditionally practiced by Christian mystics and Zen monks take the form in current Western culture of self-examination. The discipline and courage of ascetics is required to face illusions, addictions, and destructive patterns of living with rigorous honesty and make the necessary changes. In a video I saw at another retreat, the Zen priest Susan Postal offered the assurance that these changes come about more from the dropping away of unhealthy patterns than from a drastic pruning. She explained that when we observe the essential emptiness of these habits in our lives, we realize that holding on to them hurts more than letting go.

Real change takes more than meditating for a specified amount of time every day. It takes a practice of nonjudgmental attention to both inner and outer experience that comes to permeate everything we do. This kind of mindfulness is easier to learn and nurture in the quiet of a retreat setting. But the true test comes in the thick of the fray, when the choice to face difficulties or avoid them is usually made unconsciously.

The choice to be conscious can't be summoned when the need arises. It is cultivated over time in the detached observation process. Allowing thoughts and feelings to come and go without censorship or criticism builds a tolerance to what was previously considered intolerable.

A growing awareness of an unchanging reality beyond the ego self makes what was intolerable less and less a threat. A crisis might cause me to suffer, but it can't shatter me at the core, because the core itself is solid. The void that originally terrified me is turning out to be full. It is still dark — without images or words of reassurance — but it is the darkness of the tomb that generates resurrection.

Each time my eyes are opened, the stage that comes after falling apart, it is after a sojourn in the darkness. Just as a womb is essential to birth, so this gestation period seems to be necessary for me to discern the light. Closing off any aspect of life, no matter how painful, closes off connection with the source of all being. So embracing the darkness allows in the source of all joy as well.

Sometimes these breakthroughs take forms which can be disconcerting, however. On one day everything suddenly took on a dullness as if my sense perception was turned entirely inward. Then, one by one, each of my senses was restored with an extraordinarily vivid taste, smell, touch, sight, and sound. It was as if my usual way of apprehending the external world had been erased and I was starting over.

Another time I experienced an alteration in the way I perceived myself. Observing thoughts, feelings, and bodily sensations leads to a separation of identity from them. I became able to watch these manifestations in the same way I watched birds fly overhead. As a result, I lost a sense of the familiar, solid entity I had called "myself."

These temporary shifts in perception move me toward a new mind set by shaking up the way I see myself and the world. With each permutation a bit more of my blinders come off, and I have a chance at seeing a little more clearly. Each opening to a wider reality brings the peace of greater wholeness, and for a while I am living again in the flow.

The signs of the flow appeared shortly after one retreat when I stood amid the ruins of Tintern Abbey in the south of Wales. It was a sunny day in October and the wooded hills of the Wye river valley gleamed with autumn gold and amber. Only a few tourists wandered about the grounds of the medieval monastery, and for some time I was alone inside the shell of the abbey church that was open at the roof to the cloudless sky.

In the hush I lost all sense of self and was only aware of the towering stonework walls and the sun casting arched shadows on the grass under my feet. All sense of time vanished, and in my mind hooded monks carried candles in procession and chanted in the choir. I saw myself as part of the flow of all the people who had ever been in that hallowed place. I was overcome with great awe and peace.

To be in the flow is to step outside the boundaries of the

separate self and chronological time. It is to be emptied of ideas about the way things should be and therefore to be fully open to the impact of the moment. There is danger in such experiences, however, in that they are easy to become attached to. Wanting to cling to them or seek them out is a desire of the ego. When that desire appears, it is time to begin the cycle all over again at the beginning with a reminder of my aspiration. Remembering that the purpose of this quest is to empty the self, not glorify it, returns me to simple, ungrasping practice.

I did wonder about where the repetition of this cycle in my life was taking me. I found that Thomas Keating says in *Open Mind, Open Heart* that often what seems like a circular repetition of experiences is actually more like climbing a spiral staircase. "You seem to be returning to the point from which you started," he writes, "but in actual fact you are at a higher level."

Christians call this spiral grace; Zen teachers call it awakening. From the experiential point of view, the stages of the cycle come and go by just being completely where I am. What is important is the inner transformation occurring as I ascend the spiral.

I asked some of the participants at the first retreat about the changes that have resulted in their lives from this experience. Richard told me that nothing dramatic happens to him during retreats but declared, "meditation has given me a center. I don't feel so much like a reed in the wind anymore."

He pointed out the difficulty of attributing changes in his life to a single cause but acknowledged that since he has been meditating regularly, "things fall into place much more than they ever did. I seem to have gotten a much better grip on my identity in that I'm far less concerned about what other people do or think. Here I am at fifty-two, and for the first time in my life I feel as though I've discovered who I am and where I'm at. There is an inner place I'm proceeding from instead of waiting for something external to happen to me. I certainly attribute that to meditation."

For Marianne, the habitual negative thinking diminished. She reported, "Now I hear that self-critical voice and think, 'Oh, it's just that voice again.' And I don't pay any attention to it. I'm seeing thought patterns that have been making me unhappy all my adult life." She also feels that she has become less self-centered as well as able to be more open and honest with others.

Everyone I talked to indicated that integrating the experience of meditation into their lives took time. Felicite put it this way: "It's like looking through a double-paned window and only seeing a single pane. If you look long enough, something will happen, maybe someone will strike a match, that will allow you to see the two panes. Meditation is like that; you watch and you watch and you watch and all of a sudden, something shifts a little bit. It's a very subtle process."

Ada commented, "Practice can be very painful. I've cried many times from feeling hopeless and powerless when it all seems not to be going anywhere. Experiences come and go and you never know how it works. It's also hard to see the subtle development in yourself." However, Ada told me that over the years contemplative practices have made enormous changes in her attitudes toward her life and her surroundings.

Linda, who came to the retreat wanting to discern a direction for her work, was offered a job two weeks later that uses her education and experience in a way that she defines as a calling. She explained, "I didn't leave the retreat with a specific answer in my head but had a feeling that something might happen. I just continued to stay attentive and open to whatever that might be."

Several people spoke of an increased sensitivity to the suffering of others. Others spoke about improved personal and work relationships. These are signs of genuine movement of the spirit. As the dominance of the ego weakens, identity with the infinite grows and this creates an identity with others. Putting the ego in its place does not mean any loss of individuality. We retain our uniqueness as we see ourselves more and more as individual manifestations of the flow of eternal life.

For me, each time I go through the cycle, the changes produced become more and more ingrained. I am increasingly able to recognize what is happening at the time it occurs. Waking up is a long, slow process, but I see evidence of it every day in my life.

Growing consciousness is manifested at all levels of my being: physical, psychological, and spiritual. Mindful attention to my body reduces the muscular tension that builds up when I'm not aware of its existence until I'm in pain. Never again have I felt as much discomfort from sitting in meditation as I did on that first retreat. This is partly because I become aware of tension sooner and can release it and partly because my body has become accustomed to sitting on a *zafu*.

Practicing awareness of breathing and walking makes me conscious of these actions wherever I happen to be. These tangible sensations ground me in the present and reduce my mental clamor. Associations with these actions that have developed over time appear even in the midst of the most stressful situations.

Awareness of physical sensations also reveals repressed emotions, since they show up in the body. I am learning to catch hidden anger, sadness, or other unacknowledged emotions before they can overwhelm me or sabotage me by emerging in a destructive way from the unconscious. I also find that I have more energy that is not used up by tension and bottled up emotions.

Over the last three years my relationships with others have become healthier. Increased self-acceptance allows me to be more accepting of others as well. More clarity about my own feelings helps me express myself with fewer hidden messages. And interior silence makes me a better listener as well as more intuitive about what is unspoken. In these indirect ways, I am finding it possible to love my neighbor after all.

Meditation has not changed my basic personality in any way, and all my flaws remain intact. It is my conviction, however that meditation practice keeps me sane. This is probably because I am less prone to fight being just who I am. I certainly move through life with less angst, and the heavy burden of "shoulds" has lightened considerably. Inner or outer conflict causes me less distress. I act more spontaneously in the moment with less attachment to a preconceived outcome. Above all, I have a sense of movement along a path. This movement reflects the spiritual dimension in which I believe these physical and psychological changes are rooted.

Initially, abandoning familiar images and concepts of God in meditation felt like I was losing my faith. But experiencing the power of grace as well as the presence of the holy in meditation has actually enlarged my faith rather than diminished it. Because God is ultimately unknowable, this presence is perceived in darkness or "the cloud of unknowing." If God were knowable with any certainty, faith wouldn't be necessary.

My growing sense of gratitude and appreciation for simple things are manifestations of this increased faith. I no longer approach prayer as an addition to life but something that permeates all that I do. Brother David Steindl-Rast calls gratefulness "the heart of prayer" and explains that "the more we come alive and awake, the more everything we do becomes prayer." In a grateful heart I find it possible to follow the bidding of St. Paul to "pray without ceasing."

Faith is needed to allow the self-emptying process to happen in meditation. It's difficult to let go of the ego's illusion of control without faith in something to replace it. I have come to believe that self-emptying is not the terrifying loss it feels like but the poverty of spirit that leads to the kingdom of heaven.

It is possible that meditation increases faith by clearing out the debris obstructing the path to God. The debris can be created by inner turmoil or psychological trauma. It can also come from the incessant distracting din bombarding us from the entertainment industry, advertisers, and the technology of modern culture. Even religious activity that stays on the surface can obstruct a deeper awareness of the power beyond all knowing.

A consciousness grows in silence that allows recognition and response to the deepest spiritual truths. For this reason meditation strengthens whatever genuine religious beliefs the meditator already has. Clarifying one's intention in meditation determines the course of the journey. Christians approach self-emptying with the aim of saying with St. Paul, "It is no longer I who live but Christ who lives in me." Buddhists sit with the intention of encountering the Buddha nature that is at one with the cosmos. Both can find in their personal encounter with silence a spiritual renewal at the heart of their human experience.

At some point for all, spiritual insight must turn into action if it is not to become hollow. On a retreat, silence functions as a cocoon in which attention can develop. Silence protects the spirit from external assaults so that the wings of freedom can grow. But while silence can nurture the budding soul, the real test comes in the flight. No breakthrough on a retreat is as important as the resulting actions in the world. Those may not be dramatic or so outwardly different from what I did before. When I am in the flow, the ripple effect created out of the simplest act has more helpful and constructive results than the most ambitious undertaking.

Contemplatives of all faiths have in common a calling to serve others based on a vision of our shared ground of being. Brother David Steindl-Rast stresses that contemplation is the joining of vision and action. "Merely gazing at the vision is not contemplation at all," he says and adds, "Action without vision is action running in circles, mere activism."

In the Zen tradition most versions of the "Oxherding Pictures" illustrate seven more stages after the first glimpse of the ox. These stages represent many years of bringing the vision into fruition. The tenth and last picture shows a return to everyday life with the ability to respond selflessly to each situation that occurs.

In *Speaking of Silence,* Tessa Bielecki concludes her description of the mystical path of her Carmelite order in a strikingly similar way. She says, "The final expression of spousal union with God is not bed-chamber ecstasy, but the ecstasy of service. We come down from the mountain to share our life and our love with those in the marketplace."

The contemplative path must be lived moment by moment without expectation of ecstasy, achievement, or arrival. Spiritual practice is not one more activity to pursue in life but, as Ken Wilber calls it, "the ground of all human activities, their source, and validation." Consciousness is being transformed through practice all along the way. The task is to be attentive to the miracle blossoming right where we are and not go looking for it somewhere else. In this simple engagement to the depths of the ordinary, we will find what we were seeking all along.

References and
Recommended Reading

The following list includes useful books on Eastern and Western approaches to meditation as well as works referred to in the text.

Beck, Charlotte Joko. *Everyday Zen: Love and Work.* Edited by Steve Smith. San Francisco: Harper & Row, HarperCollins, 1989.

Enomiya-Lassalle, Hugo M. *The Practice of Zen Meditation.* Compiled and edited by Roland Ropers and Bogdan Snela. Translated by Michelle Bromley. Wellingborough, Northamptonshire, England: The Aquarian Press, Crucible, 1990.

Hosmer, Rachel. *Gender and God: Love and Desire in Christian Spirituality.* Cambridge, Mass.: Cowley Publications, 1986.

Johnston, William. *Being in Love: The Practice of Christian Prayer.* San Francisco: Harper & Row, 1989.

_____. *Christian Zen.* San Francisco: Harper & Row, 1971.

_____. *The Mirror Mind: Zen-Christian Dialogue.* New York: Fordham University Press, 1981.

Kapleau, Roshi Philip. *The Three Pillars of Zen: Teaching, Practice, and Enlightenment.* 25th anniv. ed. New York: Doubleday, Anchor Books, 1989. (The quotes from Zen teachers Bassui Tokusho and Daiun Harada-roshi are from this book. It is also a source for the "Oxherding Pictures" attributed to Kuo-an Shih-yuan.)

Katagiri, Dainin. *Returning to Silence: Zen Practice in Daily Life.* Edited by Yūkō Conniff and Willa Hathaway. Boston: Shambhala. 1988.

Keating, Thomas. *Open Mind, Open Heart: The Contemplative Dimension of the Gospel.* New York: Amity House, 1986.

Lee, Chwen Jiuan A. and Thomas G. Hand. *A Taste of Water: Christianity through Taoist-Buddhist Eyes.* New York: Paulist Press, 1981.

Merton, Thomas. *Contemplative Prayer.* Garden City, N.Y.: Doubleday, Image Books. 1971.

————. *Mystics and Zen Masters.* New York: Farrar, Straus and Giroux, The Noonday Press, 1967.

Mitchell, Donald W. *Spirituality and Emptiness: The Dynamics of Spiritual Life in Buddhism and Christianity.* New York: Paulist Press, 1991.

Nhat, Hanh, Thic. *The Miracle of Mindfulness: A Manual on Meditation.* rev. ed. Translated by Mobi Ho. Boston: Beacon Press, 1987.

Pennington, M. Basil. *Centering Prayer: Renewing an Ancient Christian Prayer Form.* Garden City, N.Y.: Doubleday, Image Books, 1982.

Progoff, Ira,. trans. *The Cloud of Unknowing.* New York: Dell Publishing Co., Inc., Delta Books, 1957.

Steindl-Rast, David. *Gratefulness, the Heart of Prayer: An Approach to Life in Fullness.* New York: Paulist Press, 1984.

Suzuki, Shunryu. *Zen Mind, Beginner's Mind.* New York: Weatherhill, 1970.

Underhill, Evelyn. *Mysticism.* New York: Doubleday, Image Books, 1990.

Walker, Susan, ed. *Speaking of Silence: Christians and Buddhists on the Contemplative Way,* New York: Paulist Press, 1987.

Wilber, Ken. *No Boundary: Eastern and Western Approaches to Personal Growth.* Boston: Shambhala, 1985.

Wilber, Ken, Jack Engler, and Daniel P. Brown with chapters by John Chirban, Mark Epstein, and Jonathan Lieff. *Transformations of Consciousness: Conventional and Contemplative Perspectives on Development.* Boston: Shambhala, 1986.